Dancing
on the
Wind

Poems by
Marie Scott

DORRANCE
PUBLISHING CO
EST. 1920
PITTSBURGH, PENNSYLVANIA 15238

Dorrance Publishing Co
585 Alpha Drive
Suite 103
Pittsburgh, PA 15238
Visit our website at *www.dorrancebookstore.com*

ISBN: 978-1-6491-3338-0
eISBN: 978-1-6491-3587-2

For family, friends, and you.

In loving memory of Robert.

NOTE TO READERS
Who Usually Do Not Read Poetry

Poetry can be read differently from prose. A novel or a nonfiction book is usually read from opening the first page and reading through to the last page. A book of poetry can be read in this fashion, but it can also be read piece by piece as the reader is so moved. On a lazy summer day, or in the chill of winter in front of a cozy fire, or in a pause on a busy day, a book of poetry can be opened wherever the pages fall and a poem or two can be read. A section title in a book of poetry may catch your eye. Say as you glance at the table of contents you are drawn to a love story, or a song from nature, or seeing where the writer's thoughts wandered. A book of poetry is a book that sits nearby for whenever a poem or two calls to you.

I write poetry riding the bus.

I write poetry sitting in cafes.

I write poetry at home

on the computer or grabbing a pen.

I write poetry in the middle of the night,

awakening, donning a robe, turning on the light.

When poetry stirs the blood, finds words,

it simply must be written, said.

So here it is to speak to you as it may,

in lament, heartbreak, reflection, love,

joy, observation, passion, whimsy.

TABLE OF CONTENTS

I

Singing Nature's Song

Enchantment in plain view,

this pocket of light

beneath storm clouds

above dark hilltops,

the ruffled ocean far below.

The whole sky enters the room,

an enormity of motion, shape, and hue.

I walked through the woodland park,
drawn to the color among the green—
was it the dying top of the palm,
or a bloom there?

A bloom it was, golden as sunset
tinged orange and russet,
a proud crown nestled in spreading fronds.

Then, before I could reach it,
the bus started and departed
as I hurried through the woodland
having called to me.

Disgruntled I was for having missed the ride.

Then I thought of the walk I'd taken,
the glory of the bloom.
Distress was replaced with
joyfulness singing through me.

A seagull swept
across the thoroughfare,
perched on a trash box,
looked this way and that
at the two-legged creatures passing by,
cocked its head at the grinding of trucks
and whizzing-by of cars.

Then off again
in graceful flight
back to its ocean abode
of shore and crabs
and its own flock.

My heart lifted in its flight.
So often you and I
soar into new places,
peruse the landscape,
then return
pleased with our wanderings.

DRIVING THROUGH NEVADA

White clouds billow
reflected in shadows along curvatures of barren hills dotted with nubby sage
shaped by sand and clay windswept across craggy rock.
Unexpected form etching space.

We chat.
We fall silent.
Our thoughts drift, carried on the wind, floating among the shadows.
Spacious.
Vastness of sky and rolling hills extend into snow-capped mountains.
Rolling hills, rolling thoughts.
Shadowed. Sunlit. Shadowed again.
Receding into the expansiveness of the land.

The automobile rides the ribbon of road,
carrying us to a destination capsuled within predictable confines.
Unpredicted shapes loom here,
furrows appear there,
color now,
then texture.
Deep quietness descends.
Arrested, the imagination takes flight
to where elegant thought bumps against awareness,
awakens possibilities playing at the edges of the mind.

The landscape breaks through our reverie.

We're renewed, refreshed, content.

As we roll along, joy lays hold our heart.

When first I looked,
the rim of ocean
out at the horizon
was blue as blue can be
dazzling the eye,
and closer in,
a wide swath
shimmered silver.

Out the other window
where waves crashing are visible
the sea was shining
rather than shimmering
and a jut of land
was dark against
billowing clouds
sitting atop it,
the sky gray.

When next I looked,
the ocean had turned
blue-gray from shore
to as far as could be seen,
the white breakers vivid
against steely water
and the jut of land

hazy, misty,
billows of cloud
among patches of blue sky.

And now
later still
the sun shines
on my tabletop
too bright, too hot
for further immersion
in sea, horizon,
land, clouds,
sky, thought,
too disruptive
for further pondering.

Time to close the blinds,
protect the furniture,
tend to chores,
move on
as does light
shifting
on sea and sky.

Moody, the ocean.
Give it a storm
and it roils and rages,
swells, beats its chest,
splashes fierce,
bulkheads no match for its
swishing and steaming.

Temperamental, the sea.
With kisses from sunshine
its hues warm again
sparkly and deep.
Splashes playful, now,
its white-toothed breakers smiling
for frolic at the beach.

No thin line of light today
at horizon's edge
to separate sea from sky.
Only a curtain of grey
expanding endlessly
past rain-splashed windows
past wind-rustled trees
and overhead
the same blanket
of mist and somber light
wrapping me here
in stillness.

The sea is green today.

A dark green that sparkles,

beckoning to the ocean deep

where life is sustained vast and untamed

then races white-crested to shore.

The green sea sparkling with beauty tender and sweet,

touching us with wonder and wildness

and wishes we want to keep.

Whether I'm clump, clump, clumping along

or flying, dancing on the wind,

nature whispers the songs of life,

greenness of spring, golden grasses of summer,

falling leaves, banks of glittering snow,

and always, flights of birds and the rolling of the sea.

My shadow moving flat along the walkway
revealed shape and energy in my brisk walk,
made myself visible in space and time,
physical, with definite proportions
and a particular rhythm of motion.

I watched, fascinated
to see myself in this perspective,
my actual self in reflection,
a being moving along the earth,
existing.

The leaf buds
bursts into fullness
each leaf multiplied
making a glory of the swaying limbs,
this leafy tree of summer.

The leaves fade,
shrivel and curl,
fall,
heralding the change of season,
stripping the tree bare for winter slumber.

Today in the rain flooding the streets
I saw a leaf float by,
swirling in the current,
its brown self
on a journey to the sea.

A great silence descends
as I stand in my garden
on the hill above the sea,
wrapped 'round in aloneness.
I bend to tend the soil,
weed, prune,
breathe in the fragrance
of earth and the life of plants.
A hummingbird sips from blossoms.
Sparrows and finches flutter, swoop, twitter.
The blue jay cocks a watchful eye.
All the while, tender thoughts of you.
I look out to sea
wrapped 'round in flowers, fragrance, brown earth,
and a bird watching me.

As I usually do
after pruning and pulling weeds,
planting something new,
I sit looking at the yard.

Today,
this watching ceased
and the yard, itself,
spoke to me,

the yard which lives unto itself
through every day
and every night,
the yard independent of me.

Bliss best describes the feeling
of that quiet reality of growing things
blessing me with an existence all their own,
right outside my door.

Sunlight shining on bodies of water.

Raindrops falling from the clouds.

Every snowflake dancing differently from the other.

The budding, then leafing of trees, bushes, flowers,

their blossoms bursting in thick clusters.

These are wonderful things.

Birds singing from fence posts, flying through the sky.

A bluebird eating from a hand extended from the window.

Tiny hummingbirds sipping nectar, wings whirring.

Hawks circling, pelicans in formation, seagulls swooping.

Nests of baby birds open-mouthed.

These are wonderful things.

Whales spouting. Dolphins arching above the water's surface.

Crabs scrabbling across the sands.

Worlds of life beneath the sea.

Fishes in lakes and streams, tadpoles and frogs.

Long-legged bugs speeding across still waters.

These are wonderful things.

Mountains towering above.

Jutting rocky ledges supporting giant trees.

Boulders scattered across the landscape.

Lava beds of molten rock hardened.

Vast forests oxygenating our existence.

These are wonderful things.

Fields of flowers delighting us.
Fields of crops feeding us.
Soft meadows in which to lie and gaze at the sky.
Forest paths to wander.
Mowed lawns inviting picnics.
These are wonderful things.

Clear, flowing streams.
Lakes and rivers.
Oceans encircling us.
Waterfalls.
Reservoirs of drinking water sustaining us.
Oh, these wonderful, wonderful things.

A pinpoint of light
carried at angles,
casting shadows,
highlighting imagination.

Languishes across
stepping stones
and doorways,
along buildings.

Shapes loom large,
hazy ones intimate romance,
others dance changelings,
beckon to dark caverns.

Light flickers through swaying tree boughs,
blossoms nod sunny and shadowed,
bird flight etches black across the sky,
clouds scuttle by.

Dimension and definition
in sunshine and shadow,
the day shaded with charcoal,
surrendered to depth.

Mist caresses tree boughs
casts halos around street lamps
city lights flicker in the distance
the dark expanse of ocean
sea breeze on my face
I stand at the open window
in the night
feel the whisper of you
against my skin

A tiny fly
crawling
along the petal
of the flower,
a tiny, tiny thing
living a life
alongside mine.

In the rush of traffic, the bustle of city life,

big-leafed trees dapple sunlight across the walkway

lending serenity.

A silver world laced in green.

Silver sky, silver sea, deep green forests.

It's like living in a glimmering glass globe.

Out of the mists a dark shape emerges,

at first appearing as a mirage.

A great ship, a sliver along the horizon,

a hyphen separating silver sky from silver sea

in this shining globe

fringed in green.

I watch the fog drift in,

mere condensation between colder and warmer air.

But I see the mists of Avalon

curtaining transition from the Old Religion to the new.

I see fairies dancing among sacred stone circles in leafy dells.

I see shadows of civilizations spun from these wispy vapors.

The misty veil here on my cliffs lending these thoughts to me.

I open my window
to fog hovering
at the treetops,
casting quiet
over the land,
rendering invisible
the twinkling stars.
A sharp intake
of breath,
an awakening
of sensibilities,
a sudden awareness
of this world
living its own life
separate from mine
touching me
with intensity.

Dark the night,

moon hidden in clouds.

Bright the morning,

birds flying by.

Tranquility,

as ocean rhythms lap the shore.

Lighted lampposts,
lighted windows,
hazy orbs of light
in the slumber of the night.

MARIE SCOTT

Birds soaring,
wings spread
to float on the sky.
My heart lifts,
carried from this sedentary place
to join them out in space.

They're searching for breakfast
as you sit here eating yours,
my sensible self admonishes.

But, oh, the swoop of their grace
defies intellect's take,
and my heart lifts,
my heart floats,
soars.

Sun-kissed leaves,

small, fluttery,

catching the light,

golden now in Autumn,

falling one by one,

falling on the wind,

in this Minnesota wood.

Selecting whatever caught my eye,
whatever attracted me,
I brought bushes and blossoms to my garden
and placed them wherever they flourished
with no thought to order or design.

Now just by my liking what I liked and strewing it about,
hummingbirds and bees visit,
nourishing themselves and the planet
in their flitting and buzzing,
their curious delight.

Clouds gather.
Great masses of white and gray
swarm the dark headlands,
fall into wide white ribbons
and race along the bay.

And something in me rises to meet them.

My feet rooted with the
towering cliffside cypress,
my joy and wonder
take flight,
billow,
roam free.

In a field gray and dying
a lone tree stood
orange and golden
against the autumn sky
shouting the glory of sunset.

There is no way to get lost
in these acres of gardens
with well-planned pathways
as towering trees, shrubbery, nodding blossoms
call me into the quiet majesty
of the life they're living,
losing me completely
in their richly-scented world.

Silly to rhapsodize
birds and flowers
clouds and breezes
the rolling sea
the mighty forest.
Sentimental. Trivializing.
But when they speak
it is only polite to answer
as best we can.

Floating, or seeming to,
the looming clouds
darkened with moisture.
Coming fast behind them,
a great chariot of roiling clouds
filled with light, tinged with shadow.
And below, the pale green-grey sea.
Cliffside cypress sway in the wind,
sung into a dancing frenzy
rain-washed at midnight.

Green, the lush grasses
brightening shadows beneath the trees.
Trilling voices of birds
newly come for nesting.
Blue skies.
Puffs of clouds floating by.
'Tis Springtime come again.

When leaves flutter
and branches sway,
when rivers run rushing
and breakers scurry to shore,
then you know the world's alive
and that you are in it.

All morning—

Green forest

Gray sea, gray sky

Ships and people passing by

The air is soft this morning,

and still,

mist from fog

spots my glasses,

dampens my hair,

kisses my cheeks.

The earth may quake,

buildings may tumble,

civilizations turn to dust.

But in this moment,

the sapphire sea

touches the soul,

and waves crash to shore.

The spicy scent
of fresh flowers
reaches into quietness,
gentleness,
fragrance.
I am stilled,
made whole,
not having known I was scattered.

TWILIGHT

Softly it comes —
dusting with darkness
the eventide —
whispering tenderness
to our embrace.

II

Words Dazzle

Words dazzle me.

Words catapult from my mind

or saunter forth with a grin of satisfaction.

Words from others, spoken or sung or springing from the page

stir my imagination, provide food for thought.

Words can erupt in hatefulness, violence, hurting, harming.

But here, I think of words that carry into the moment

or propel into deeper inquiry or wrap one in gentle solace.

Without words I would die of thirst,

starve from hunger,

stagger through life emaciated.

With words I sing in harmony,

dance with the stars,

rotate with earth.

Words bring me into alliance with the human race,

touch my heart to yours.

The language of life
where gods do not reside
or if they do, do not harken,
is the language of poets
whose words cradle
the murmurings of the heart

There are writers and there are readers.
Most writers are readers.
Some readers are writers.

Words spill from writers,
millions of petals, seeds of thought
swept into the winds of time,
words precious to readers.
"Can't be too many words," they exult,
basking in the glory of them.

And writers whose words spill from them,
who can't stop the flow of words,
words pushing to be written, pushing to be heard,
act as scribe, enlightening,
bringing intimacy with the human spirit
into the minds of readers, into their lives,
into their expressions in the world,
into who they are and who they become,
in how they touch each other as a people.

Readers and writers!
Giving form to our existence,
our collective awareness,
our hopes in the present,
our dreams for the future!

The cadence of words shifts and changes.

There was a time when poetry rhymed.

Now is a time when it doesn't always.

There was a time when songs were crooned,

then they were stomped and shouted.

What is this invisible rhythm

flowing through hearts and minds

tapped out on keyboards

scrawled across paper

shaped collectively

into differing tempos and styles,

shifting peoples, shifting nations,

this invisible rhythm across time.

Writ large we are
in the pages of books.
Writ to know who we are,
us people, you and I.

Poetry is mostly snippets,
a glimpse here, a glance there,
glimpses into a day, into life,
glances at the starlit night.

Picking up a book of poems by Billie Collins,
it occurred to me that if my poems were to be published,
in "About the Author" noted at the end of that unlikely book,
"Poet Laureate" or "distinguished professor of literature" would be absent.
Instead, it would read "an ordinary person with no credentials whatsoever."

That might be something—
to have the ordinary words of the likes of you and me printed on august pages,
telling of our lives, our thoughts and feelings, our heartbreaks and victories,
our imagination, tenderness, perceptions, shouts of exhilaration and outrage.

Not that we wouldn't welcome Billie into our company,
with his laureate and scholarship,
his poetry a contribution to literary excellent,
the poetry of a real poet stirring our hearts.

While we're at it, let's invite Ellen Bass to join us!
She, too, comes with accolades, puts words in ways we simply cannot,
her poems reaching into our lives,
warming us, enriching us, inciting us, exciting us.

We could let our own words join theirs,
gentle offerings of we ordinary-people poets.
the writing of words in the quiet of nighttime to steady us, teach us,
prompt with greater ease our ordinary trudging along.

And who are the ordinary people of whom I speak?
I can think of three: Cynthia, Janice, and me.

A murmur of words,

warm voices across moonlit waters.

A pause.

The world hushed

in the murmurings of lovers.

III

Those We Grow Up With

Whispers of the holiday season of yesteryear!

Childhood and sledding,

falling snowflakes outside frosty windows,

Christmas trees from trudging through deep snow in wild forests

come indoors strewn with popcorn and tinsel,

the jangle of festivity, the gaiety of laughter,

secrets of gifts, angel wings in the snow.

Frill and frolic wrapped 'round the years.

Whisperings brushing our hearts with tenderness.

Family myth-making. The halo effect.
The dismissive remark,
"Your mother always saw things in a rosy light."
My heritage. We were raised on stories
of myth-making proportion with a halo effect.

I'm an old woman now,
my mother and husband both dead,
much of my life lived, the good and the bad,
with life still stretching before me,
and I see the wisdom in that myth-making halo.

The disappointing, the lesser-than, the irksome,
the ugly and disastrous, the hurt of real wrongs,
all those facts and behaviors that erase
our innocence and harden our hearts
are all too obvious, all very much with us.

In the fertile ground of cynicism
grows an expectation of the worst.
In our actual experiences
of the badness in every one of us,
the rosy side can be hard to see.
The stories of family myth-making
call attention to the better in us,
balance the equation of what can inspire us,
sustain us, enrich us, give us a rosy glow

by which to find a way to our own kindness,
by which to harken to the best in us,
emboldening courage, holding us steady,
making us part of something
which is rosy, worthy of myth-making.

"Puff the Magic Dragon

lives by the sea"—

his little five-year-old mouth

puffed in a perfect O,

voice ringing sweet and clear.

These are the moments inscribed on the heart.

"What is your name?"

asked the gracious woman they were visiting.

"Frey," he said.

"Why did you say your name is Frey,"

inquired his mother, later.

"Because I'm always called Jeff

but never Frey."

Moments ringing sweet and clear.

"Owe," came the cry from the attic.

We ran in alarm.

"What's the matter, Jeffrey. What's the matter?"

As he came crawling from beneath the rafters,

"A woof bit me!" he wailed.

A nail had pricked his tender skin,

pierced his world of imagination.

Moments, moments.

The uncle played the game of mis-naming
with this little boy.
"Pigs," the uncle would say,
pointing to the sheep.
Peals of laughter from the three-year-old.

A man, now, this Jeffrey,
riding in the car with his uncle.
Passing a pile of dirt heaped high,
Jeff said, "A field of daffodils."
Peals of laughter.

Moments inscribed on the heart.

The last grape jam.
Least favorite of all.
Strawberry, raspberry, peach
Always chosen before grape.
There's raspberry in the freezer,
Even now,
Saved as best for last.

This grape jam
tastes like nectar,
Its ruby red color
Piercing my heart.
I look at it,
Ruby red, ruby red,
Each time I open the lid
To dip it onto my bread.

And the taste.
It doesn't taste like
Least favorite grape jam.
It tastes like
Summer sun on lush clusters
Of purple grapes hanging
Heavy on the vine
Among the misty hills
of Sonoma Valley.

It tastes like
Ancient goddess times.
Hanging gardens.
Wonders of the world.
Ruby red.

It tastes of my mother,
Of time turning.

Re-used cottage cheese cartons
Stacked in her freezer
Full of jam.
"Take some jam," she would say,
when we'd come by.
"Are you ready for more jam?"
This jam is the last jam
That my mother will make.
She's giving up the task.

In these later years of her life
The jam she made
Was freezer jam.
In our growing-up years
It was jam stirred on the hot stove
Along with a pantry full of canned fruit,
Peaches, pears, apricots, tomatoes.

Growing up
We had a garden
In the back corner
Of the cow lot.
Summer evenings we'd all go out
And pick raspberries, strawberries, vegetables.
Mother, us four kids,
Even Daddy when
He wasn't on the road
Driving truck
To earn us our living,
Mother stretching the dollar
With sewing and canning
And selling milk from the cows.

And now this jam,
Last of the grape jam,
Setting me to thinking
Every time I have
A piece of toast.
Setting me to feeling
Something warm, something changing.
Catching my gaze with the vibrancy of its ruby red.
Stopping my taste dead in its tracks
So that I'm tasting,
Really tasting,
This grape jam.

And at the edges of my mind,
Out the corner of my eye,
A tiny old woman
Smiles at me.

Her soft skin
I've rested against my whole life.
Her quick blue eyes
So bright, engaging.
Her mouth laughing.
Talking, always ready with a story.
Her lips pursed in thought.
The tip of her tongue tracing her upper lip as she sews.

A tiny old woman
Haunting me with memories
Reminding me I'm alive
Reminding me I'm hers.

A tiny old woman
Loving me.

Ruby red.
The last of the grape jam.

Nasturtiums orange and bright and rambling
drape their vines along the rock wall of my garden
and I think of Daddy. They were his favorite flower.

I think how I would love for him to know
that after he was gone
I visited the land where he grew up.

I think how I would love to tell him
that his father's middle initial stood for Roy;
he was, indeed, named for his father,
just as he'd hoped he was, this father he never knew,
lost to him at two months old to the day.

I think how I would tell my father,
who all his life through did not
know how his father died,
that on that fateful day,
it was an accident which took his life away.

My father's uncles were there, at the time of the accident,
cousins of his father there with his friends, buddies.
I would tell my father that I learned of this
in their account written into family history
which I uncovered in my search of where he grew up.

I think how I would tell him
that I am now acquainted with the names of his cousins,
sons and daughters of the uncles who were with his father,
how I know they played together, were part of each others' lives.
I would tell him that I know their significance in our family history,
their significance to him.

I think how I would love to hear the stories he has to tell
about those cousins and that place and that time.

I think how I would ask him
who the two women were in the tall house I remember
from the trip we took when I was twelve
to this land of his childhood and young adulthood.

I think how I would tell him
that if he could tell me who they were,
then I would know how those women and that house,
important enough for us to visit,
impressive enough for me to remember all these many years,
fit into my life story.

I think how I would tell him
that I remember the picnic given in his honor on that visit,
and I would ask him who all those people were
who came to see him after his long years away.

I think how I would tell him
that I had learned his mother was adopted at birth,
that his grandmother was the sister of his mother's mother.
I think how I would learn from him if he knew this.

I think how I would tell him
that through his grandmother on his father's side,
he can be proud of lineage in England
traced back as far as the 1400s.

I think how I would tell him
that our ancestor, William Cantrill, Gentleman,
came to America in 1608, to Jamestown,
the first permanent settlement of English-speaking people.

I would tell him this ancestor is named in the Virginia Charter,
that he accompanied Capt. John Smith of Pocahontas fame
in the discovery of Chesapeake Bay.
That Cantrill's Point, located along the seacoast
between the Potomac and Rappahoannock Rivers,
is named for him as it's English discoverer.

I would love to tell him this
because he did not know of it
and was mistakenly under the vague impression
that shame was associated with family arrival to these shores.

I think how I would love to tell him
that his family history continued with names now reclaimed
and is part of the long story of those who
settled our country into what it is today.

I think of his shy smile
that would touch my heart if I could share this with him.

I think how I would love for him to know
that it is in fond memory of him
nasturtiums grow in my garden.

Tolerated my loving family,
at times childishly declaring if I wasn't related
I'd have nothing to do with these people—
even as I drove long distances to visit.

Now, being part of those to whom I belong
wraps its arms around me,
love usurping tolerance.

Three butterflies
fluttering, flitting,
alight in Paris,
soar the Seine,
circle cathedrals,
hop on and off buses,
hover in souvenir shops,
their bright wings opening, closing.
High up Eiffel Tower they fly.
Lightly they wend their way
through neighborhoods,
into theaters and cafes.
If you listen carefully
you'll hear the tinkling of the laughter
of these tiny creatures in this epic land,
Beverly, Cynthia, and Marie,
butterflies three flitting
in the gaiety of Paree.

Sisters four are we.
We've played together,
fought together,
grown up together.
Got old together
through the shifting patterns
shaping our lives.
And in all this time
in all this liveliness
the silver thread of love
weaving us together
shimmers brightly.

Marie Scott

I watch this sister mine
as she gathers clippings from the yard
tossing them into the compost bin
rolling it to the curb.

I watch this sister mine,
the little girl running and playing with me,
the young woman on her way to Paris,
the sister returning home to marry,
the wife, the mother.

I watch this sister mine
gathering clippings, rolling the bin,
an older woman now, this sister mine,
sister through a lifetime.

She wrote letters.
Not often.
But now and then
as occasion arose
letting others know this and that.

The years passed
and a time came when her letters
were recovered.
The pleasure of recalling was hers,
hers to savor, hers to share—
a train trip across Canada
from Vancouver to Ottawa,
love letters,
her mother visiting her in Paris,
correspondence from and to
family, friends, her children,
a special Christmas letter
at the birth of her first grandchild,
a special letter
upon the death of her mother.

Touches of the riches
in living her life.

When I visit, as I often do,
I always stay with one sister
of the two who live in town.
But the occasion arose
when I stayed with the other
who prepared a room for me
with joy in her heart,
wrapping me 'round with love,
this sister who comes to visit me
at my house
where we romp and play and
sing our sister-hearts' warm song.

She was Ruthie,

this little sister our ours,

with her red hair

as aflame as her bright spirit.

As a young woman she became Ruth.

It is she who said, "He likes you,"

to her clueless older sister,

spotting the brother-in-law he would become.

It is she who brought to us

our beloved first grandchild, first nephew.

It is she who entertains us with her love of fun.

It is she who seriously looks to life's meaning.

It is she who moved to Hawaii

where now we visit our Ruthie, our Ruth,

in the land of flowers and sea.

Each sister giving birth.

The life of the family expanding.

Each new one touching our hearts.

Lifelong hugs and kisses.

Here, unexpectedly, the rhythm,
the rhythm of being in step.

Us family here together
listening, talking, warm glances, laughter.
Something deep inside
touched of its own accord
without need of anything more,
in this rhythm of being in step.

John points as the moon
seems to travel through the clouds.
We smile at this and feel the rhythm,
the wasteland of loneliness vanishing.

Evergreen trees green again,
the waving of grasses a delight,
birdsong sweet, breezes gentle,
as the heart expands wide as the rolling seas
in the rhythm of being in step.

The day of the dead.

A fake skeleton sits in a chair at an entryway.

Reminding me.

Apparitions float toward me.

I see Mother, her lively spirit, bright eyes.

I see Daddy standing beside her with his shy smile.

Robert opens his arms in a loving embrace.

Nate is with Ruth reflected here across the waters from Maui.

Suzanne and Julie are laughing at my surprise.

Richard rushes to Lorraine.

Gary! There *you* are.

I see Jim's back as he turns to greet Sharon.

Oh! Kirby meets Bev at the door.

Fanciful. Comforting.

This day of the dead.

We living, remembering.

It's things, sometimes, which we glimpse from the corner of our eye
that shape our lives in contours otherwise not expected.

Sitting as a seven-year-old in the women's lounge in Sears,
my legs sticking out in front of me in the too-big chair,
women with hair styled differently than I was accustomed to seeing,
wearing dresses and shoes different from my mother's,
smoking cigarettes and talking in an offhand manner,
intriguing me, capturing my imagination.

Going to dinner in a house with dark wood paneling,
eating at a table elegantly set,
tablecloth heavy and luxurious, glasses that sparkled.
And afterward riding in the car down a hill where lights glittered,
unknown to me in my flat-lands neighborhood outside the city limits.
A caressing within me which I hadn't known existed,
didn't know was being massaged into a warm glow.

Walking along the streets, shopping downtown,
people all around began shouting and hugging each other.
A stranger bent down to me and cried,
"Oh, my darling, isn't this a glorious day! The war has ended!"
I was five. I didn't even know what war was.
But in a flash of brilliance running through my body,
something immense apart from all I knew was suddenly mine.

These were aberrations to my upbringing, a lurch from the ordinary
flitting across my awareness within a second of my existence,
tiny unheralded events unregistered as part of my life,
not even known to have occurred by my vigilant mother.

They left a trace upon my consciousness, a snail's trail to follow.
They let in a world larger than I knew, a *beyond* that called to me.
Other factors conspired to carry me, albeit not brilliantly,
from colloquial thinking to intellectual, from parochial to literary,
from rural to city, from religious to secular.

These later factors, however, engaged my mind, heart, body
separately and rationally as opposed to startled breathlessness
which, without my knowing, captured me in my entirety.

I was only seven and in the lounge for a matter of minutes.
I was in grade school when I had but one meal in an unfamiliar environment.
A five-year-old when abducted by thrill running through the populace.
I'm now 74 years old and have thought deep thoughts, felt deep feelings,
gained perspective on the world.
Yet the color and movement and impact remain
in being taken unawares by sudden opening vistas.
I marvel that such un-marvelous moments can be so marvelous.

I watch, now, at what suddenly, unexpectedly, unobtrusively
draws the attention of children, and even of adults,
in a way that makes their eyes widen.

IV

Fanciful

If I were a painting
I'd be golden lilies nodding in the shade.
I'd be the sky-blue sea
rolling soft white waves onto sandy shores,
or maybe an ocean dark and wild
splashing against rocky isles.

If I were a painting
I'd be slashes of red and gold,
swirls of indigo and rose.
I'd be fine lines of arches in random intersection.
I'd be thickly layered
in purples and emerald.

If I were a painting
I'd be a city skyline of twinkling lights at sunset
and lovers sipping wine.
I'd be starlight and moonlight in a midnight sky.
I'd be you and I.
If I were a painting.

There's a tiny place within me, emerald green,

that sings the sweetest songs that have ever been,

sounds that melt me into waves of light

and send me out to a universe bright

where I float and fly

and dream large and small

and know things I've known

and things yet to know.

There's a rhythm, a beat,

that's soft and neat,

that's wild and free,

that's safe and great,

and I rest in that sound,

I run and I leap,

I spread wings that shimmer,

I soar and I glimmer.

I swam in the ocean
with fishes and crabs,
tangled with seaweed,
was spit up on the sand.
Pelicans bombed waters bulging to waves,
and seagulls cried high in the sky
as I lay sprawled on the shore
with the sun in my eyes
and my heart gleefully
singing for more.

The leaves of the willows aflutter

The rising wind in my hair

Horses galloping, tails high, mane flying

The rolling meadow beckoning me to run

Run

Run

Gasping for breath

Blood coursing

Exhilarated

In the howl of the storm at my heels

I'm a little squirrel

who wraps her bushy tail

across her sleepy eyes

and nestles in her warm bed

come the early dark of winter,

opens her bright eyes to the light,

nibbles on her garnered stores

and leaps from bough to bough

for romps in the frosty morning air.

Trapped, swimming,
not unpleasantly,
in waters with no outlet to the sea.

Some days the sun is warm.
Other days,
fog wraps its arms around me.

Day breaks.
Slipping into the water
sends ripples.

I dive. I splash.
I move, agile, graceful.
I lie on my back and watch the clouds float by.

I come to shore,
nibble fruits and berries.
I sleep in moonlight.

Trapped,
not unpleasantly,
in waters with no outlet to the sea.

Slender the legs of the horses
lifted high through dust and shadow,
the moon looming on pathways
through dewy meadows,
bends slick with waterfall spray
rounding into glades of verdant forests
etched with rocky ledges,
the slender legs of horses
trotting spritely, brightly,
carrying me to you.

If I were a grape
would I know
that my life was progressing,
moving from forming on a stem
to growing purple and plump in the sun,
to being plucked and hauled
among million of others, packaged,
set on grocery shelves, and now
washed ready for eating?

Would I, were I a grape,
feel like I feel as a human,
each stage a normal course of things,
growing up, coming into myself,
bundled together in human endeavor, growing older, dying,
all the experiences of life unfolding?

Would I, if I were I a grape
knowing I'll be eaten,
be no more frightened than
a human,
knowing I'll be dying?

MARIE SCOTT

Before me stood the Goddess of History.
In one hand she held the sun and the moon and the stars.
In her other hand she held the Earth.
Catching my eye, she slowly twirled that glorious blue sphere
to reveal Thought Forms which have entered human life.

Thought Forms shaping this ever-changing world,
emerging, mingling, contradicting, disappearing.
The collapse and the rise of empires and cultures
as the life of Thought Forms shift, change, burn-out.
Thought Forms colliding, polarizing, causing turmoil,
enlightening, leading forward.

The Goddess of History shifted the globe closer
and I could see the human mind and heart.
The brilliance of her gaze sharpened until I saw how
it's up to us.
It's up to us
to carry us where we want to go.

As my eyes brightened and my thoughts
circled like the sun and the moon and the stars,
my heart beating wildly,
the Goddess of History reached out her arms
in an embrace of tenderness and tears.

V

A Love Story

I love you more than God, she said,

she who loved God with her very life,

as she gazed upon this man who lay next to her,

lean and strong and beautiful.

She never dreamed in all her girlish daydreams

that loving like this, the reality of it,

the manliness of it, could so overtake her.

And he, hearing her words,

seeing himself reflected in her eyes,

softened into loving like he'd never known.

We didn't notice
we were luxuriating in pleasure.
It was just normal
to luxuriate so.

It looked like billowing cotton,

the white fluffiness into which we flew,

but bumpy it was,

currents hidden from view,

and I thought,

This is how it is living with you.

Then, bumping along,

I thought with a smile,

And here we are, in it together,

billowing softness and whatever.

How did this slim film of cellophane
slip between us, halt our full embrace,
our cells poised, our skin touching,
our bodies hugging the contours of our hearts.

How does the fragrance of your neck, your hair, your breath,
hardening my nipples, lighting me with fire,
bump against invisible walls,
smash against crushing forces.

Though Ginsberg HOWL and Wollstonecraft rage,
the violation of our sensitivity,
the shattering of connection,
outpace Time itself,

leave you and me,
O my beloved,
weeping
for each other.

Her tears were disconcerting to him,
he never quite knew what to make of them.

Sometimes the tears came from
the beauty of the love-making,
the overwhelming intensity beyond any other kind of touch,
the sensation of knowing each other.

Sometimes the tears came from
the absence of connection,
distance exposed by pretend intimacy,
embrace closed to the aliveness of exchange.

Whichever way the tears came,
they spoke of the unspoken
and he didn't know what to make of them.

He curls around me
as we crawl into bed,
the top of his foot soft against my toes,
his warm breath in my hair,
cherished.

Here is the tender, vulnerable side of this man
whose gaze shifts into the distance at the mention of war,
saddened, haunted, these many years since,

who glances away, face closing,
for an instant all movement stilled,
when spoken to in sharp, unexpected tones,

whose face opens in the company of a child,
delight dancing into his life,
his expanding heart broadening his chest.

Here, the barely visible side of this man
cries for recognition but daren't ask for it,
longs for a way to open into a safe place,

resists seeking arms to hold him,
lips to speak kindness, smiling eyes.
My arms, my voice, my eyes,

within which, every once in a while,
this man trembles slightly,
then with a tiny sigh, laughs, happy.

It caught my attention.

My thoughts were elsewhere when suddenly

I more felt it in my solar plexus than actually heard it.

But I did hear it.

I heard her say to him, "I think you're one who lives a double life."

"Do you live a double life?" I now ask.

"No," he says.

To myself, I say, "I think you do.

I think you pretend to love me

and then you live alone in yourself."

She meant something different.

She was speaking of deceit.

At least, I think she was.

Although I wasn't really listening

and only heard that one sentence

because I felt it in my solar plexus.

I think it means something.

I think it means I know something I don't know I know.

Something that plagues me, haunts me, keeps me wondering,

startles me when I least expect it.

Not the way to live.

But I live this way because I want him to love me.

Because his pretending to love me, if pretending it is,

—just his pretending—

is delicious, so wonderfully delicious.

Its sweetness softens my heart, warms my soul, delights my life.

So I ask, "Do you pretend to love me?"

"No," he says. "How could I sustain pretending for all these years?

I don't have it in me, and more to the point,

how could I fake having such fun with you?

Loving you is where it all started and where it always is.

That's where no one else came close.

If I didn't love you,

how could all the ways you annoy me be so insignificant?"

Which makes us laugh. Such a good feeling.

So now I don't know what to do about that feeling in my solar plexus.

But I do know I'm happy for his words.

Rarefied, the air,

this sea-splashed morning

with the sun brimming on the horizon,

my heart singing,

your eyes as blue as the sky,

the warmth of your smile,

the touch of your hand

illuminating my life with pleasure.

O, this delicious, rarefied morning.

You're still here, the server said,
as she returned from her break.

Oh, yes! we replied.
We got to talking.

I'm not rushing you, she said.
It's good to see you enjoying yourselves.
So many married people sit silently reading the paper,
eating without looking at the other.
But you, you always have something to say.
And you laugh a lot. It's good to see.

We do. We love eating out for these very reasons.
To sit across from each other relaxed and easy.
To talk with each other like we talk with no one else,
speaking of things as they strike us,
sharing items of interest that we've read,
making observation about things going on around us,
looking at each other, covertly touching,
sparking around private jokes, warming to fond memories,
debating politics, social issues, life choices,
planning, reviewing, celebrating the day.

Nothing in all of life better
than us together.

Where it exists in relationship
we embrace.

Where it doesn't
we relinquish.

Then we keep truckin'
together.

That's trust.
That's love.

I am thinking of the movie *About Schmidt*
played by Jack Nicholson and Kathy Bates,
and living a moment in-between.

If I weren't so resigned, tears would squeeze from the corners of my eyes.
Instead, as Kathy Bates said, I put my mind to
"vacuuming the flour off the floor and hoping I don't die."
That is, I think how I can make the day work.

He has asked what we'll do today.
It's New Year's Day. He's looked out the window and said,
"It's a new year out there!" before crawling back into bed.

He's wanting to have fun.
He starts questioning shall we... do you want to...
I cringe. Pull away inside. Feel how the attempts to be
with me come from other things than... Something Else.

Then the Schmidt moment happens.
He knows I've pulled away. I feel him pull in.
We lay there as if nothing happened,
as if we're still waking up to the New Year and having fun.
It's in that deadness, the tears don't come.

Last night, after the movie *About Schmidt*, he said,
"Every man is plagued by Schmidt's question of what his wife thinks of him,
of whether she is disappointed in the man he became."

And I said, "There is a difference between men and women.
Men seek being valued by what they do and who they are.
They can't get past that indoctrination,
and their disappointment is inconsolable, their isolation is impenetrable.
Women don't have the luxury of anyone caring what they become.
And they don't care about what a man becomes.
They don't even care about what they themselves become,
whether homemaker or career woman or both or any other thing.
They care about what it is to be with another.
They care about being there, themselves."

After the movie *About Schmidt*, he wondered about Schmidt's reaction
to the drawing of the six-year-old from Tanzania.
"What was he thinking?"
"He was feeling," I said. "Feeling someone reaching out to touch his hand."

We lie here now, all the truth of Schmidt
a heavy weight on our chests, a knot in the pit of our stomachs,
a despair in the center of our hearts.
We lie here next to each other miles apart.

"I want this to be your day," he says, after a time.
"It can't be my day," I say.
"I have to think about how to make it right for you."
The indoctrination she can't get past.

"I don't want you to do that," he says.
He touches the tip of my nose. I cringe. I brush his hand away.
I hate him to touch my nose. He knows that.
I know he's trying to be with me.

"This is a Schmidt moment," I say.
"It is," he says.

"What was the movie with Al Pacino previewed last night? he asks.
I remember Pacino but I don't remember what the movie was about."
"It's about him training a young guy for the CIA and saying you never
know how it really is, or something like that," I say.

"Let's get up and go see an early show of *Catch Me If You Can*.
That's a movie with Jack Nicholson playing Leonardo DiCaprio, Nicholson's
     that good."
"Yeah, and Kathy Bates plays Tom Hanks whose really Al Pacino
because you never know how it really is."
And suddenly, here it is, that... Something Else.
How did that happen! That wonderful thing between us!

"So what would you do if you could do exactly what you want to do," he says.
"I'd write a poem," I say. And so I do.

Schmidt still lays heavy on our hearts.
We'll try hard not to forget to remember not to live him.
We'll fail. It will be awful. We'll bear it.
And then that... Something Else will remind us.
That's where we've got it over Schmidt.
We're persistent in bearing it side and side.

"I love these
bursts of happiness
between us,"
I said,

as we sat in a favorite cafe
in our favorite city.

And with smiling eyes
he replied,

"Me, too."

The night
when all seemed lost,
he said, "I feel badly I can't meet your needs.
I feel inadequate."

I said, "You're not inadequate.
I'm just not who moves you."
He said, "There isn't anyone to whom I would respond.
I don't know how."

"If that's so," I said,
"we can begin again.
We'll go slowly and be careful."
"I want to," he said.

I touched his cheek.
He didn't look away.

Outbursts.
Fierce, angry.
Lashing out all the pent up
hurt and frustration,
defeat and distancing.

Each of us insists, in the lulls,
that we talk, work this out.
What's happening?
What's needing to happen?

Speaking. Listening.
Putting dialogue into practice, empathy.
Flaring up. Retreating.
Speaking more clearly.
Listening openly.

"I'm afraid of you
When you're so angry at me."
"I *am* angry at you.
What do I mean to you?"

"I don't know."
"That is the question you have to answer.
It's your not knowing
that I'm so angry at."

"I do know, if I can find the words.

You are intelligent and kind and fun.

You are who I am eager each day to be with.

You are who I love deeply inside myself."

The anger in me subsides.

The fear in him eases.

Our bodies relax.

We stay present,

to each other and ourselves.

We venture movement.

Drop the schedule.

Let go of the plans for the day.

Move from moment to moment,

alert as to how we can be with each other.

Do this. Go there.

Attempt to accomplish that.

Stop when harmony falters.

Talk with each other. Be quiet together.

Find our balance.

"That man over there.

He does to her what I get angry at.

His eyes don't include her when he looks at her.

Now see her and the woman with them.

See how their eyes include each other."

"I see.

I understand.

It's a habit.

A stance.

Now I know what makes you angry."

Alone together,

he touches his face to my chest.

His body softens.

He rests a moment.

We smile.

And later,

he grabs me,

looks beyond me

at the football game.

We laugh. This is what it isn't.

Could your heart sing free,

would it sing of me?

Were you to be spun in my direction

would your embrace reach for mine?

As the stars dance across the sky,

would it be to me you would dance to see?

Would this sweet caress you give me now

be your caress through the course of time?

O pleasure in every heartbeat.

Wonder in every smile.

Could it be?

Your heart forever singing free with me!

We taste better

in our youth

and feel better

with our flesh firm.

But with age

a tenderness follows,

an appreciation for life lived,

when the hand caresses

and lips touch.

Traveling life together.

That's what came swimming into view

in the blue of your eyes smiling into mine,

the blue of mine smiling into yours,

spinning us into what makes us undeniably us,

our gaze warming our hearts anew

in the loveliness of traveling life together.

We kept finding where love abode.
When expectations crumbled
and the claws of disappointment
scratched gouges in contentment,
when our view of each other
shifted to chasms we hadn't seen before,
when affection floundered,
when the swirl of life around us
carried us where we didn't know we'd go,
bewildering,
his strong arms would
wrap around me.
I'd feel his breath in my hair.
I'd glimpse him, still and somber
as he matched my pace and I his,
having found where love abode
in all its many guises.

VI

Sorrow Visits

There are times
when you collapse into the moment
and let it carry you,
each day given to its service.
This is one of those moments.

There is only the changes
that can't be real
yet insistently persist,
every day a dusty whirl
drawing you somewhere.

His body so thin, his pain so constant,
so impossible that it can't be true
even as you give it succor
with all that's within you.
Even as it becomes everything.

Your tenderness grows.
It envelops him,
envelops you,
floats you both
on this sea of uncertainty.

Tenderness moored to your heartbeats.
Tenderness in the embrace of your arms

strong from holding him fiercely
against whatever is upon us
that has him in a terrible vise

clutching him between life and death
before our astonished eyes,
our trembling souls.
He clings to you. He relies on you.
You cherish him.

The heat of the disease
so foreign, so unfamiliar
rests against your skin,
the skin of this awful moment
swelling beyond your grasp.

The birds have stopped singing.

The ocean is silent.

The wind is stilled.

Blossoms have closed.

My Robert is gone.

I wrap tightly around myself
and move carefully in small steps
through familiar days
foreign
with him gone.

There might be a fire.
Be prepared for an earthquake.
There's always danger of an auto accident.

Platitudes pronounced among us
tossed into the wind.
But now,

now that illness swooped down
and carried him away,
the casual remarks startle, shaken.

Rolling along the tracks
my mid-section tightens
at the train wreck that could be.

Ready to be home? someone asks,
and my house in flames
flares into view.

Houses on the hillside
crumble into sticks,
tumble into the sea.

The shining sea
rises treacherous
washing us all away.

Once vague improbabilities,
vulnerability clutches me
raw and real.

In my stunned sorrow,
possibilities once remote
become a tremulous certainty.

The blue jay swooped onto the branch,
tipped her head toward me,
tipped her head toward the plaque
I had just placed on the ground beneath the tree,
reading, "You are gone yet not forgotten."

The blue jay flew to the plaque, hopped all around it.
Quickly she pecked it and stepped back, pecked it again,
then pounced on it with both feet,
lifting one foot then the other
in a somber dance.

Into the tree she flew and placed her gaze upon me.
She then landed near the place where I sat,
tipping her head from side to side, eyeing me.
Back to the tree for a look at the plaque, at me.
Then away she flew.

Of your remembered self, dear Robert,
Happy Initiation by our blue jay
whose parents and grandparents
feasted on our holly berries
as we watched from our window.

Or do you suppose, my love, that she was saying,
"What a ridiculous thing to place in our yard,

nothing to eat from it or to build a nest.
You humans with your strange ways."

Or perhaps, as Cynthia suggests, she was saying,
"Wow. Check out this fancy dance floor.
Can't wait to tell all my friends
how cool this human is!"

Whatever it may be,
I'll always think she danced on your grave,
my darling man, my love,
saying, along with me, her
goodbye.

The house is empty now
with only me within it
to sit in the scattered remains of departure,
regrouping.
My thoughts flit then coalesce
drawing together the cluttered remains,
shaping a space of substance and sustenance,
to tingle on my skin,
ease my heart,
move me onward.

I walk carefully

between the open drawer and my chair at the table.

I cross the room without stumbling,

placing my feet with care,

the exhaustion of loss,

its disorientation,

tugging at equilibrium.

The hollowness of life once filled with light

casts gray circles around my heart,

my feet uncertain

between shadow and the new ground on which I walk.

I would sometimes be embarrassed
when he and I would often
walk down the hill to the restaurant.
It seemed we'd be seen as strange
to frequent so routinely.

Afterward, now that he's gone,
it doesn't bother me
to go often, even more often.
Not sure why.
Am I seen as the lonely widow?
That would be embarrassing.
Am I seen for my friendliness?
That would connect me to the human race.

The curious thing is that
how I am seen doesn't matter.
My walk down the hill, turn left,
walk the block along the cliffs to the restaurant
morning after morning
and sometimes afternoon, too.

It is just what I keep doing,
afterward.
And I like it.

Watching television
Just as Robert and I did
The programs we enjoyed together
Engrossed, exactly as it was

Then with a jolt
I realize I'm watching alone

I'm sitting on the couch by myself
I'm sitting in the room by myself
I'm in the house by myself

Today I wore his dark green wool v-neck sweater.
A Christmas present from me several years ago
costing more than usual,
something really nice.

I glanced down to find a small white hair
tucked into the weave of the warm wool.
I reached to brush it off as I'd done so many times before
in all those sweet years when his hairs would fall.

I caught my breath,
my fingers poised.

Here it was still,
his hair.

There it stayed.

When light blends into sunset
and stars begin to shine,
when the moon floats into view
and I think of you,
there's a pause in the rush of time,
a heartbeat moment of memory
as nighttime fills the space
once filled by you.

I can be walking down the hall
on an average day
normal as normal can be
and suddenly I'll feel struck down
with the realization that
I am no longer part of him nor he of me
That he is no longer with me.
I think this will always be.
The rest of my life is not long enough
to move forever away from him and me.
To live without him is to walk with a limp.
It makes my heart hurt each time
that I'm minding my own business
and am once again struck,
struck down by the thought of it.

When the sun comes out
after you're gone
and the blush on the rose
can cause my heart to sing,
then I know there's a song
deeper than the sea.

I don't always want it to be so
clinging as I do
to the song that was you,
but then there's the moonlight,
and on waking,
the shining of the day.

MARIE SCOTT

Fear flickers through me
Uncertainty
Your arms wrap around me
I'm safe, once again.

Fear flickers through me
I am alone
I remember your arms around me
I'm safe, once again.

I must no longer make you a frame of reference,
my beloved, so dear to me
that all I want is to have you by my side
even in your absence,
seeing life as being with you still,
observing what's around me
as if you are with me.

Okay to feel you near,
to share my thoughts,
delight with you were you here,
just because it always was
and still is so very much fun,
but not to make you who and where I live.

I catch myself grieving for you, my body aching,
in seeing life as with you still,
the disconnect of your departure
which is real and inconsolable
leaving a gap in my heart, a gap in my day.

I must separate from you.
O, my Robert. Not forget you.
Remember you, hold you dear,
but no longer identify myself with you,
no longer see myself as belonging with you.

I must belong only to myself, now,

or live in a space of longing never to be filled.

I must discover that unfamiliar space

which is now my space alone.

Going about life without Robert,
here I am in the airport
with all the unfamiliar push and pull,
lugging baggage, trotting from here to there,
interpreting signs and symbols, finding my way.

Doing it all myself.
To be sure, with the love and caring at my back
of friends, sisters, a devoted nephew and niece,
but here, in the airport on my own, I'm taking it on.
Without Robert. With surprise.
A surprise to be moving through the world so.

I do see the world differently,
this being in charge instead of following along.
I see the shape and course of things,
alert to how to navigate, how to get from here to there,
aware of my surroundings and how things work.

I learn skill in the things he knew.
I had knowledge of them,
but they were not within my repertory of concern and initiative,
waiting as I was upon him to lead the way,
keeping with his rhythms.

Surer-footed this change in positioning. Clearer-sighted.
More at ease when all is said and done.

Not distracted by instructions, comments,

by attuning to moods, perspectives, opinions, wishes not my own.

His steady hand then, though, transfers to my composure now,

a compass to my making my way gracefully.

I'm liking this taking the fore.

Lost, however, the strong arm to lean on,

the pleasure of simple exchanges,

the warm smiles between us,

me and him in the world together

embracing each other, embracing life.

This I miss. O, how I miss it.

I'm seated at Park Chow, Robert.

No longer is granola served with mixed fruit.

No longer does anyone here know us.

The music is as loud and noxious as always.

The service is just as bad.

The people whose order was taken at the same time as mine

were halfway through their meal when my single Marion's pancake arrived.

It was delicious.

You would be chomping at the bit.

I love the irritation on your face, your annoyance

that I can't have what I always had when you were here,

the waiting, the noise. You'd dump them, now,

despite the dark-wood cozy ambiance, the dancing fire.

With such affection, I miss your grumpy self,

seated here at Park Chow.

I bring the softness of your blue sweatshirt
to my lips, along my cheek. I close my eyes.

My laughter at something on TV has you sitting beside me,
my heart atremble, resonant of our shared laughter
through the years, side by side.

Your smell is laundered away, now,
as I wear it still warm with the thought of you,
how it draped softly against your chest,
how you pushed up the sleeves, your strong arms endearing me to you,
how it hung, at the end, from your slight frame,
oh, you, in your blue sweatshirt.

I stood at the kitchen counter
scooping out papaya,
sweet and juicy,
and found myself remembering.

With our hamburger on chapati bread
we ate papaya.

I stood staring at the whole papaya I'd be eating
instead of the half that was mine in our sharing.

My mouth watered but
my heart softened and wept
for wanting you here.

I spread the cherry jam onto the scone.
Glance at the jar—glance at the scone.
Enough scone left to finish the jam?
Probably not. There's a dab in the jar
beginning to sugar around plump delicious cherries.
Ruefully, I say to myself, Typical.
Before us, the whole end of our life together,
and you die.

Sure, it had begun to sugar around the edges,
age creeping in,
but oh,
that dab of plump delicious life
still left for us.

I was having a conversation—
people familiar that I couldn't
place as I lay half-awake
in the between time of consciousness—
and the lament enveloping me
in a haze of agony and yearning
was that he had gone—
after the rupture—
turned away and never returned.
I felt astonishment
that he would just turn and go—
then I remembered—
the rupture was death.

There are moments when I linger
with what was.

I look out the window and you are here
watching with delight
the flocks of migrating birds
and our resident blue jay
feasting on holly berries.
No birds, no berries, now,
the holly tree sickening and dying
at the same time as you.

Sitting at my dressing table
I see you reflected in the mirror
at the sink behind me, shaving,
and tenderness washes through me.

I lotion my body
and suddenly pause
in the treasure of your caress.

Flying to Oregon you are peering out the window
that I gaze from, now,
and I feel again your love of the fields in springtime,
your happy anticipation of bright blossoms
and lush green forests.

For an instant as I don a jacket for an ordinary occasion,
you enter the room with your old eagerness for adventure,
to be on our way, to find a spot not yet visited.

I'm moving on.
New routines, new adventures replace ours.
But there are moments when I linger
with what was.

I twirl on tiptoes and make graceful leaps.
I think you are watching, smiling beneath your mustache.

I dance lively across the full expanse of floor.
I think of you laughing.

Dancing new steps not danced before,
dancing familiar steps learned long ago,

I think you are pleased to see me dancing.

It was for a lifetime.
But a lifetime was just for awhile,
this special time together,
ours to love each other.
It wasn't for forever.
Life doesn't last that long
and lives don't end at the same time.
So it was just for awhile
that we had each other to love.

Thinking it was for my whole life through
is what keeps me clinging to you,
thinking it was for forever,
was all of me, this being with you.

Now from a poem I heard that rang true
my heart can tell me it was just for awhile
and it wasn't all of me
that special time together,
that time we had to love each other.

My girlhood wasn't my life.

Being a student and a career woman wasn't my life.

Robert wasn't my life.

Each of these times was the part of my life I was living then.

Being a woman alone isn't my life; it's what my life is for now.

I'm a person living a whole lifelong.

Goodnight, my love.
I'll see you in the morning.

I'll see you in starlight,
I'll see you in the rising of the moon.

I'll see you in the little girl skipping alongside her father.
I'll see you in the little boy pointing at the bus going by.

I'll see you in every mountain peak,
in every stretch of road,
in every new place to wander through.

I'll see you in a cup of coffee after trudging through the city.
I'll see us arm in arm walking our hillside street.

I'll see you in our nearby cafe,
in the smiles of those you greeted,
in the warmth of those who knew you.

I'll see you in the swaying of the trees. I'll see you in the soaring hawk.
I'll see you as the blue jays squawk their territory
and the hummingbirds shoot into the sky.

Goodnight, my love.
I'll see you in the morning.

Oh, my beloved.

I would spread my hair across your chest.

I would lay my cheek upon your breast.

If only I could, if I only could.

You would twine your fingers through my hair.

You would touch my face with whispered breath.

If only you could, if you only could.

Our hearts would break.

Our hearts would soar.

If only we could, if we only could.

VII

Me, Myself, and I

There is the deepest quiet
here, living alone,
deeper than I've ever known.
When I walk across the room,
the denseness of the quiet
wraps 'round my ankles.
Light as fog, breathy as wind,
it lifts to my innermost,
my mind freeing, my self releasing,
even with my heart aching.

I live in a world,

a world of doorways,

of rooms arranged to taste,

of windows filled with sky

looking out over ocean and rooftops,

neighboring houses stacked on hillsides.

I live in a world of walks through Cypress forests

catching the light between towering trees.

I live in a world of restaurants and shops

in the bustle of city life, full of ideas and activities.

I tend to business, balance income and expenses,

see to household chores.

I live in a world of friends near and far,

of family held dear.

I live in this small world

encompassed, contained,

rendered comfortable in quiet pleasures.

Riding the bus among strangers,

I sit, a small, undistinguished person,

and think to myself, how extraordinary

to live in a world.

I love this city.

I love the special spot where I breakfast most mornings

bringing to me a piece of the whole world.

People working here come from Mexico, Japan, Ireland, China,

Puerto Rico/Honduras/Chicago, the Philippines,

and today, a tall blond of European descent.

Peter from Vietnam, recently retired,

left an opening this new person will fill for ten days

until he's off to study at the Sorbonne, alma mater of his mother.

A party of customers having finished their meal stop by my table

to say they are a group of "Lefties"

who meet as friends and relatives of the Abraham Lincoln Brigade,

of which I've never heard, Americans who went to Spain to fight Franco,

to fight the fascism creeping it's way into the world again.

On another day a man from BBC here for a conference on climate change,

discussing the lesser-noticed results of our climate changing,

brings new information to my attention as I eavesdrop.

I love this city,

its richness extending to the bottom of my hill.

To smile at storybook pathways
winding through narrow forest
on cliffs above the sea, blue or storm grey,
white splashes of surf against rocky shores.
This is home to me.

To stand at parkland's edge
and gaze at green, green grass
spreading beneath forests of trees.
The scent of eucalyptus.
This is home to me.

To board the bus into the city bustle,
sustenance of livelihood,
entertainment with friends,
cradle of life with a beloved.
This is home to me.

To tuck indoors,
other houses and mine scattering the hillsides,
wide windows opening to a sky of sunshine
or quiet wisps of fog drifting by
or shape-shifting billows of stirring clouds...
and the sea.
This is home to me.

MARIE SCOTT

The eagle soars,
the hawk spreads its wings,
filling the heart with wonder, with poetry. Magic.

Not magic. Science.
The soaring of the hawk is a measurement
of velocity, air mass, and other innate variables.

That same science
measured the degree of reality
held by the optimistic and the depressed.

It found that those who are depressed
have a more realistic grasp of situations
than those who are optimistic.

But I am one
who plunged the depths of depression
and resurfaced.

I am one who knows
the other side
of depression,

and it's life soaring,
it's wonder at the sight
of eagle and hawk.

It's not the ocean so much that I like
as living at the edge of the world.

Tucked away in my mild manner and conventional ways
is a stirring for the edges,
the edges of thought that launch new thought,
the edges of feelings that pull toward deeper ones.

It's not the ocean so much that I like, though like it I do,
as standing where earth ends and stretches of space begin,
where the winds from the sea and the cold from the deep
meet the warm air of land.

I wrap the view from the window around me,
the ocean, fluttering eucalyptus, stately spruce.

I submerge myself in the novel I'm reading
which teaches me of lives unfamiliar.

I let the silence of the room
envelope me.

This is a day of reaching downward
into the stillness of my own life.

As of a certain age
or at a certain time,
it just ain't gonna happen
that someone steady and strong
will join their life with yours.

So as of a certain age
or at a certain time,
you bolster your courage,
call on your cheer and
strike out on your own.

Superfluous.
That's what I'm feeling
this sun-drenched morning
with a blue jay sitting on the fence.
Superfluous
in a world mired in muddle,
everyone needing something,
deserving something, something better,
as I idly kick a can along a dusty path,
stop to put my hand to trivia now and then.
Trill on, blue bird,
tipping your head just so.
O shining sun, warm my stilted heart
in your golden glow.

When I begin writing bad poetry

I know the moorings are loosening

and I'm afloat in a sea of possibility.

I feel the swells rising,

the storms gathering.

There is an opportunity
Which lies in a quiet place
Then someone says this
And someone says that
And someone asks something of me
And I forget

Each day life happens
and I'm happening in it.
Soon
I'm all wrapped up in it,
life,
and I like it.

In the ablutions to begin the day,
in the splashing on of makeup,
I looked into my own eyes
and in that pause saw myself
clear and lively, unhurried, here.

In the shining waters beyond the treetops,
in the stretch of sky and the color of the sunset,
I looked into the eye of the evening
and in that pause saw this world
bright and fresh.

In these pauses of actual seeing,
I looked the depth of light in the eye
and saw the quiver of life
and me in it
whole and coalescent.

Played Big City today.

Strolled the street lived-on

where first we felt the Big City Life.

Feeling grand, bought an overpriced piece of clothing.

Had lunch with a glass of wine.

Stopped short of the glamour

of calling a limousine for the ride home.

Clamored onto a bus instead,

another symbol of Big City life,

limousines, buses, rare or non-existent

in the small towns from which we'd come.

From the bus window, glimpsed the many people,

the astounding architectural variety, felt the thrum.

The thrum of the Big City.

Where now I play.

I woke from a dream of Robert flirting.

I don't care if he's dead.

He doesn't get to flirt.

Laughingly, I told this to Janice.

"This is funny, sweet, and melancholy all at once.

Write it down. It's a poem or a piece of one," she said.

So I did.

I fall asleep
wrapped in the night.
Stars circle my head,
the moon at my heart.
I slumber serene,
cradled in quiet
swaddled in dream.

I awaken to
sunlight warm on my face.
Stretch into the daytime,
move my body with grace.

I roam free,
alive to the pleasure
of living this life
that's at hand.

I woke up listening.
I heard the caroling of birds,
a symphony of tones and rhythms.
I heard cars passing by,
breezes rustling the trees,
the neighbor's music,
their door opening and closing.
I heard within me a murmur of discontent
with my plans for the day.

Rousing myself to push on
I felt a hollow place
in the pit of my stomach.
I laid back down. I listened.
Won't do it today
these plans I've made,
not up to them.

I heard a great noise.
A large truck stationing itself
in front of my driveway
to unload enormous
cargo for next door,
its huge iron arm
lifting high into the sky.

I couldn't leave in my car
if I wanted to,
blocked in as I now am.

Just then my phone rang.
He with whom I'd made
plans must go into work unexpectedly,
postponing our plans to another day.

I heard a murmur of contentment,
the rhythm of the day unfolding in its own way.

Who is this sprite
who tumbles words to me
which dance and sing and ponder
and ease my fretfulness?

When I feel wavery,
uncertain of who I am
or what I'm doing here,
I see my mother's face, my mother's life,
with her bright energy and indomitable spirit.
Then I can see the world as ever-opening,
as ever-mine to be met with vigor,
to be embraced with optimism.

When I feel wavery,
uncertain of who I am
or what I'm doing here,
I let myself feel myself standing on the earth.
I imagine myself silhouetted against the sky
tall and lean and strong.
I feel my breath coursing through me.
I fill my senses with all that's green and vast and golden.

It was strange enough
that bedridden with depression
I felt myself floating down,
down and down,
so deep as to be endless,
then floating back up again.

It was strange enough
that having floated up
there would be a feeling
of quietness, peacefulness
and I'd get out of bed
and wash my face.

What is strangest of all,
it's been 40 years or more
and never again has depression,
a previous frequent visitor, visited me.
Strangest of all is the echo of joy
within me through all these years since.

What a relief when

just as slumber descends

thought expands

to where perception

and words and ideas

are of the same quality

as clouds and sunsets

That curious pleasure
of being alive
just for the pleasure
of being alive
is mine.

Like a whiff of perfume,
a soft breeze,
a gentle caress,
it makes it's presence known.

And I find myself smiling
in this lightness,
this filling of me with gladness
at simply being alive.

VIII

Whimsy

A journalist at the *Chicago Post*

said of *The Prophet*, penned by a poet,

"a singing in the heart as of music born within,"

The Prophet so singing making a poet of a journalist.

I'm pretending I'm a Beat Poet from the '60s

as I sit here in a coffeehouse

although not on Telegraph Avenue

nor in North Beach,

not a coffeehouse like any then,

this with its upscale commercialism,

its architecture repetitious across the City,

its lack of intellect, its lack of a beat.

But the maple and walnut scone is delicious

and the coffee will do

and as I pretend—

the walls waffle,

the sound of voices take on a timbre not heard today,

music insistent fills the space

where my mind let's go cold and clear

in the beat in the thrum of yesteryear.

The world has shifted for us.
The invention of the safety pin was a wondrous thing,
a thing outside the common imagination
but not outside the ability to comprehend.
Anyone seeing the safety pin
could see that with the bending of wire
it became a new thing.

A toothbrush with the word "sonic" in it, however,
which sends impulses that destroy plaque
is another matter altogether.
No-one of common knowledge can discern its making.
Neither do they understand
the thing called "plaque" it's destroying.
The world has shifted for us.

Pin-curled and permed
and cut short
was my hair.
Then as I budded
from being a child
I looked in the mirror
and said to my hair,
"No more. I declare
and make promise.
No more pin-curls and perms.
You're now growing free."
This I said to my hair,
I was saying to me.

In this moment
my life is in a lull,
meaningless in terms
of aspirations,
meaningful in terms
of kittens dozing
in the warmth of the sun

She couldn't just walk alongside her mother,

the little girl, such a tiny sprite.

She had to skip,

had to jump over the white stripes of the crosswalk,

gaily swing her bag

in the happiness of this walk with her mother,

the happiness of going somewhere

in her red coat

on this spring day.

Do you remember being that young!

When play was your whole world.

When you could run like the wind

and hold your breath under water.

When stories were magic worlds

and your mother and father chased away monsters.

When angst was fleeting, given way to fun.

When danger was climbing a tree and disaster was non-existent.

Do you remember being that young!

When the bus passes by a sign
advertising the life of Bill Graham
who put rock 'n' roll on the map,
I smile. With shared names
Billy Graham was preaching against the devil's music
while Bill Graham was promoting it.
We must be in America!

It's a balancing act,
this knowing where you are in life,
balancing from within yourself,
and within the ebbs and flows of your day,

when you're thriving,
connected to others and to intentions in meaningful ways,
when you're adrift,
meaningful others no longer at hand, intentions vague.

It's a balancing act,
this standing first on one foot, then the other,
finding your place within your own heart,
finding your way in the world—

before letting it all go,
ensconced on the couch
a good book or stories on TV,
then tucking into bed.

Always thinking,

always devising constructs,

ways to be in this world.

Which is good.

If we didn't

we wouldn't have a way

for our empty toothpaste tubes

to disappear.

Discussing tooth care with my dentist
I mention I use toothpicks.
"Older people tend to use toothpicks,"
she said, and gave advice against their use.

It never occurred to me that toothpicks had a life span,
would lose their status as instruments of hygiene,
like so many things we took for granted having disappeared,
dial phones and phone books, parking meters for a nickel
instead of an arm and a leg, instead of no meters at all,
automobiles your dad could maintain
now computerized beyond comprehension,
clothes pins and lines for drying clothes,
safety pins, even, by and large—
you need to hold something together,
you toss it and buy a new one.

And me, myself, with a life span,
not the person who uses toothpicks
but an older person who shouldn't.

TO SHARON

Two old women
as frisky as colts,
and just as wobbly of leg,
as prone to quick naps.

So, I think,
this is getting old.
Not bad, I think,
as she puts the key in the ignition
and I place my finger on the map.

There are no attics,

no houses passed down

through generations of families,

attics where great-grandmothers,

and great-great grandmothers' elaborate dresses

and hats with big feathers are stored,

where aunts and great-aunts' poetry

fills old-fashioned notebooks

packed away in boxes beneath the rafters.

How will we know the pleasure

of dressing-up in their clothes, their dainty button-up boots,

with the scent of their life in our nostrils?

Without old photo albums tenderly stored,

how will we learn the names and faces

of those whose faces resemble ours,

that line of family in this wide, wide world?

How will we know where feet have trod

treading the winding pathways

to the perimeters of where we stand

pointing to vistas not yet traveled?

How will we know the landscape

of our destiny?

How will we?

With no more attics.

Yesteryear and shining today collide.

Where those in the household

turned back the clocks or leapt them forward

come or go daylight savings time,

clocks today,

clocks on computers, smartphones,

electronically hanging on the wall,

turn of their own accord.

Understood, taken for granted by the young. Ordinary.

Startling to some of the rest of us

catapulted into today.

Who says we old folks

don't have a rip-roarin' good time?

We aren't "tearing up the town," as the saying goes,

with our creaking bones and delicate digestive systems,

but our laughter is uproarious,

our stories are seasoned with years of relished living

and we know how to listen and when to speak,

the flow of conversation spinning a web of sparkling intricacies,

for aliveness is precious to us as we teeter on the threshold,

and we treasure the warmth of friendship and the reckoning of good times.

We old folks! We know how to live.

We've had the time to hone the art.

Once upon a time
you would pile into the car
and drive downtown
where you'd shop
for a piece of furniture
needed or desired or both,
delighted to add something new.

You would find just the right thing,
pay for it and drive back home.
That same day a big truck would arrive
and men would unload the furniture
and bring it into your house.

That was once upon a time.
Today, what you see in the store
that you wish to bring to your home
will be handed to you in pieces
in a box you'd think could never hold
the large wonderful thing you'd just purchased.

You have to lug the heavy box home,
and then you have to tug and pull and struggle
to take out all the pieces and fit them together
to construct the item you saw in the store.

And if you think that's an easy task, think again.

More often than not it wobbles and creaks,

isn't nearly as sturdy as you thought it to be.

And getting it put together!

More curses can be heard in the effort of assembly

than are heard in a whole month of day-to-day living.

Oh, where has it gone,

that once upon a time.

ACTUALLY AND TRULY

There is an accountant
whose name is Greenbach

And a handyman
whose name is Wrench

How wonderfully
perfectly delightful is that

Two pigeons caught my eye
flying low atop the line of traffic.
They lighted on a lamppost
and I laughed as their heads turned this way and that.
I could imagine the comments they were making,
the humorous observations on life down below.
Then they flew away together,
and that they were together seemed tender and true.
I noticed the lamppost was covered with droppings.
It would seem it is often they stop to chat up what's new.

You think things will last your lifetime,
bathroom fixtures, pipes throughout the house,
the deck your husband built stained in sentiment.
But they don't.
They crumble with time.
If you're smart,
if you're strong and courageous,
you'll toss them without a care
and welcome the new that's there.

The WWII wartime poster displayed a woman with her
blouse sleeve rolled up high on a muscle-sporting arm.

The "wartime girls," however,
working men's jobs as "their part in the war effort"
were figuring out how to avoid getting muscles
and to hide them if they did.

A generation later, girls who have not known war like that,
girls now called young women
with no jobs any longer exclusively men's or women's,
all jobs—all the world—theirs,
clothe themselves in tank tops and leotards
and work-out in gyms to "sculpt" their muscles.

Times change.
Change with times of stepping out,
stepping out of where we've always been
and flexing a muscle or two.

IX

Letting Thoughts Wander

To have a singing within
that is bells and lilies and birdsong
sunk deep in restfulness—
that is a true blessing.

The global sphere is home; the wide world mine.

So what's this heart-tug when Scotland's soil I roam?

What are these teardrops come at the sound of pipe and drum?

Is it the green, green hills and high highlands?

Is it the stories dramatic and bold?

Is it the cry of courage and love of freedom?

Or is it the tender haunting of kith and kin from ages yet untold?

As we on this side of the world slip into soft slumber
and those on the other side of the world rise to begin their day
we do so altogether on the earth circling round the sun.

We struggle. We fight. We harm each other.
We suffer terrible hardships.
We play for power. We rule and are ruled.
We think we're obliged to certain ways.
We love one another.
Our hearts sing. Our hearts break.

And all the while
we're living on the earth
as it circles around the sun.

Steam curling from hot coffee
while rain streams down
washing dust from leaves and windows,
dimpling the surface of the lake.
The heart softening.

In the company of others,
lots of words, little connection,
except for the human spirit
softly circling, warming contact.
The heart rejoicing.

Ranting and raving on the state of affairs,
letting loose a healthy harangue
met equally with more complaints
until we're laughing.
The heart releasing.

A sudden moment aware,
the air quietly filled with being
in the midst of everything,
standing solid and whole.
The heart singing.

Presence in the ordinary,
in the movement of the heart

touching into wonder
not want to be missed.
The heart strengthening.

As I walk down the hill leading to the sea,
I hear the sharp urgent moan of a ship's horn.
A ship coming to harbor.
I scan the horizon.
Not even a shadowy glimpse can I see
in a fog eclipsing it bow to stern.
Through that dense atmosphere, that gray whiteness,
a great vessel moves invisible,
only the sounding marking its existence.

I stare at the shrouded view,
and think of a ship, of waves,
of ocean depths teaming with living things.
I think of me walking in sunshine on the cliff above the veil.
Shall I write a moral to the scene,
or maybe some profound observation?
No, I'll simply see the invisible ship in a sea of fog
and feel the cool air on my skin.

Haunting, it was,

the music coming from someone's player.

The haunting that reaches into the depth of one's being,

stirs memory and dreams, excites the senses,

fills up empty spaces of longing, sends one on their way

with a sweetness encircling the heart,

making extraordinary this ordinary moment

of riding a city bus.

Everybody is assaulting everybody
with ideas, opinions, passions,
chatter from the mundane to the profound,
from the profane to the sacred.

I do it.
I'll wager you do it, too.
What would it be like if none of us did it?

I'm thinking we'd smile more.
We'd listen better.
We'd pause to think more thoughtfully.
We'd engage with each other
in what is right here between us
instead of in heady fragments of nonsense
spilling out our mouths.

And here I am,
assaulting you with
my opinion!

Getting older
there is a leathery quality
to our senses.

We taste the air.
We see the brilliant color
trace the horizon.

It's easy to become
callous, hardened, embittered,
disgruntled, pessimistic, joyless.

Jaded. We've seen it all,
and in large part,
promises anticipated, unfulfilled.

It takes
careful concentration
for our senses to burst alive,

to tingle
and dance
and carry us away

on the ecstasy
of living, breathing
wonder.

It takes
a moment
of catching our breath

for the crust
of dusty pathways
and disappointed aspirations

to drop away,
freeing our eyes, our ears,
our nostrils, mouths and skin

to receive
the delight that's
just as plentiful now

as when our newborn,
childhood, youthful
selves

took in
the world
around us.

It takes
attention
to open ourselves again.

MARIE SCOTT

Every generation turns morbid,
disillusioned,
sees the world turning for the worse.
So it is with me.

But I question my perceptions,
remembering when an earlier generation
saw as disastrous
what I saw wondrous.

Joy is a subtle thing, different from happiness.
Happiness is a flash of light, a splash of colors.
Joy is abiding, permeating, enveloping the core of being,
tempering emotion, harkening to the more that may be,
bringing assurance to the experience of being alive.

Joy surfaces in the flight of a bird, the nod of a flower,
the lapping of water on the shore.
Surfaces in the kindness of strangers,
the warmth of a lover, the sweetness of friendship.
Quietly emanates through unease, loneliness and fear.

Or so it is for this person with the privilege
of having a loving family past and present,
of being in good health, having a home and income,
of not being harrowed in a war-torn land,
of not being racially or religiously attacked,
of not being hungry.

Does joy enter the lives of those under such extreme distress?
Is joy the ingredient, the subtle, pervasive element,
which makes life endurable in the throes of agony?
I don't know, but I wonder,
for how else can the suffering of the world be survived
without something like joy innately touching the human heart.

MARIE SCOTT

Let us sit before our mirrors
and reflect upon attributes we wish to define us.
Intelligence will surely be one,
our ability to think, to reason, and more,
our ability to assess the potential in our reasoning,
to look upon the world and draw connections
between what is familiar and what is new,
what serves the good for all and what does not.

Let us sit before our mirrors
and let grow in our minds attributes which shape us.
Education must be included,
informing our intelligence with facts and figures,
with context, perspective, history,
with frames of reference by which to see patterns,
teaching us where we've been, how we got here,
teaching us to learn from one generation to another.

Let us sit before our mirrors
and see clearly who it is that we are.
Humanity must be added.
Caring about our own selves enough to hone our best,
caring about others enough to nurture compassion,
all of us proudly teaching the values of our varied cultures,
the value of each other in the making of this world.

Let us sit before our mirrors

and see in our reflection where we stand.

Self-awareness is a worthy attribute,

where it is that we stand confident within ourselves,

how it is that we stand trustworthy in relationship to others,

perceiving how broad our sense of being is

as we fit into the scheme of things.

Let us sit before our mirrors

and see ourselves reflected.

Love is an attribute to guide us,

guide our every thought, every action,

imbue our existence, inform our best intentions,

embellish our imaginations and sustain our efforts,

to make life worth living,

to give meaning in seeing our way through the day.

MV Code Club: We Teach Kids to Code.

What in the world is teaching kids to code?

Tidy Shoppe. I have no idea what a tidy shop is.

Culture is getting ahead of me!

I do know what Home of the Whopper means,

and Gordo, my favorite taqueria for burritos.

I remember when my parents were my age,

how things commonplace to younger me were unfamiliar to them,

and how they began to confine themselves to the familiar.

Maybe next time I pass the Tidy Shoppe and the Code Club,

I'll go inside and acquaint myself.

It matters how we live, I realized,
the blossoms along the walkway smiling at me,
blossoms scattered from seed by a thoughtful neighbor
who loves nature, loves beauty,
offering these blossoms to enrich our lives
with whimsy, brightness, lightness, delight.

The jolly sight of them for some reason caused my thoughts
to turn to the admirable characteristics of rescuers
in war-torn countries and natural disasters,
"decisive, fast-thinking, risk-taking, independent,
adventurous, openhearted, rebellious, flexible."

I think of the courage of sufferers of injustice.
I reflect on the differences between activism
which seeks to liberate, raising the voice of those unheard,
and activism which deigns to control,
imprinting a hierarchy of privilege.

It matters how we live.
I thank my neighbor who planted bright blossoms
along the walkway of our safe and pleasant street,
brightening our days, tweaking the happy hopefulness within us.

Laughter sparkled between us,
the corners of our eyes crinkling.
Talk sparked back and forth
loosed from restraint, spontaneous, free.
Friendship it was, true and real.

You do more than
prepare and serve food,
provide clean utensils,
have coffee cups at hand.

You brighten lives.
We customers come
in a celebratory mood,
come alone or with friends,
come for the ocean to call to us,
and there you are.

Without ever knowing it,
each of you,
in your own special way,
brightens our lives.

Aaron Brown.

I know his name from its lettering on the vest he wears,

the vest he wears as he helps build the building across the street,

the vest he wears as he comes to the gym

to build his muscles for the hard work of building buildings.

Aaron Brown and I exchange glances, smiles,

recognition that though he doesn't know my name,

that though we don't know each other at all, we share existence

working-out in the same room together at the gym.

A day will come when Aaron Brown

has finished building the building across the street.

We'll no longer exchange smiles.

But through the happenstance of time and space

we have shared a slender moment,

this Aaron Brown and me.

Conversation, by and large,
is everyone, me included,
translating what is being said
from our own thoughts and opinions.

A way of listening, I'm thinking,
that keeps us stuck,
thought rotating around in our heads,
bouncing back and forth among us.

Assuring never-ending sameness, it seems,
our lot as a species—
maybe not never-ending,
change does occur.

But oh so slowly
we embrace each other
in new and expanding ways,
open to understanding one another.

In the morning light and shadow, from across the street,
a cylinder appearing to tumble down the side of the house
is actually the irregular angle of the roof.

A bright flower fluttering against dark soil
gives a strong impression of a dog bobbing its head,
then as no dog would stand so long in one place
I have to re-assess what I am seeing.

I blink at the sight of a two-headed man.
Then the person standing behind him moves aside.

From my perch on the cliffside I spy a small boat out on the Bay,
until a movement reveals it is actually a hovering hawk.

Misperceptions, bringing to my attention
the importance of seeing clearly,
of basing understanding on reason and factuality.

So now I find myself looking twice,
asking others what they see,
thinking things through again,
laughing at fondly held beliefs.

Some valiant efforts hide hidden snares.

Some save against disaster.

We stumble along, progress into unknowns.

Cherish us for our fragile attempts.

Hold us dear in our good intents.

I declare,
the function of the news
it would seem
is to let us know
that things aren't as peachy-keen
as we'd like to think
and there's not a thing
we can do about it.

Well, I for one,
despite the news
which I do not doubt
is reporting trouble true
am looking for peachy-keen
and lo and behold,
· I'm finding it
just about everywhere.

Oh, do let us find that place
to stand in this world
where when the hammer strikes the bell
it rings clear and true.

When we look
at a person,
catch their eye
and smile,
something
warm
happens
for both of us.

I sit looking at the world within easy view from the window,
a warm cup of coffee in hand,
thinking thoughts of no consequence, dreams elusive,
the stuff that consumes the day between work and play.
Molding me, here, startling me, making me glad or sad,
this seeing the world, thinking dreamy thoughts.
And a thought I have is of you.
You, too, do you sit with coffee in hand,
thoughts unaware shaping you anew?

A sad old woman,
they called her,
sad as in pathetic,
sad as in mournful.
In both meanings of the word,
they say with their eyes and solicitude,
they say behind her back,
sad old woman.

Striking fear in the heart of old women alone,
excommunicating them from the thriving throng,
relegating them to the unwanted,
their verve, resilience, charm unclaimed.

Tumbled in the surfs of time,
rising dripping and sputtering,
a veteran of love and sorrow,
she, perhaps beyond everyone else,
knows the alchemy for shaping life.

While she trudges on, full of spit and vinegar,
carries wisdom and humor within her gray head and tender heart;
while she is a favorite aunt, cherished sister, beloved grandmother,
rich in friendships, with interior life of pure spun honey;
while she welcomes each new sun in the grace of existence
and strolls her day in the finery of life well-lived;
these renegades of ignorance spurn her beneficence, her beauty.

Sad, indeed, their loss of humanity,

these purveyors of prejudice and harm—

for hurt she is in such unwarranted dismissal.

San Francisco!
City where we move our bodies
and free our minds,
ascend to hilltops,
descend to the sea.

San Francisco!
Wrapped by bay waters
islands and piers
caressed in ocean breezes
cypress standing tall
doorways ensconced
in bougainvillea brilliance,
the scent of wildflowers.

San Francisco!
Lively San Francisco!
Awakening the senses.
A city
shouting
joie di vivre!

A tiny dog trots along,
his smile witnessing his pleasure.

A tiny bird perching high in the tree
trills her song and awaits its answer.

A tiny glance in my direction
gladdens my heart.

A tiny thousand things tease and tingle
each and every always.

In stories
people get to be seen,
heard,
told out-loud.

In life
the joys and heartbreaks,
quiet adventures,
moments of victory
are lived in normal day-to-day,
seen as unremarkable,
heard as ordinary,
narrative of plot
and character unrevealed,
never told, never spoken,
quiet nothingness obscuring
the wonder, verve,
customary courage of
living a life.

Then comes a tenderness
at the doorstep of our living,
a tiny thread of color:
mothers telling stories
of childhood sweetnesses,
ancestors and old times.

You and me
seen, heard, told out-loud.

To find the breath within the moment,
the kernel of sweetness in a thing,
that is the secret to happiness,
to the world taking on shape and color.
That is the turning of the mind
from loss and loneliness
to joining with life and living.
That is being alive.
That is when we can dream sweet dreams,
reach out our arms to embrace others,
ride on the wind.

When nothing takes hold,

not the urgent distress of the nation, of the world,

not the variety and excitement of the City,

neither career nor family, not philosophy or religion.

Nothing.

When nothing takes hold and wandering begins,

what then?

What then, when flesh is aging,

when fashion and sparkle hold no allure,

when thought finds nothing worth thinking

and feelings lie mute,

when routines overtake engagement

and visions of lollipops dim?

Is then the time to sink into quietness,

to walk softly and look around,

greet passers-by with kindness,

feel the flutter of breezes

and notice clouds passing by?

Is this when life disengages

and living serene begins?

how amazing

consciousness

how truly, blissfully astonishing

to know we're alive

to think across time

knowing present, past, future

to feel coolness and heat

to feel ecstasy and tragedy

joy, terror, anger, tenderness

to know love and sorrow

beauty and ugliness

to let them inform us

to recognize green leaves budding

floating clouds, bright blossoms

to hear the ocean, the call of birds

the wind in the trees

smell all the scents of this great world

to know this life of which we're

amazingly, astonishingly conscious

The artist moves from mere reproduction to deeper dimensions,

brushing strokes of perception,

expression beyond the form, the scene,

hue and shape enlarging, sharpening.

The author, wordsmith,

waits for the unexpected, waits for just that right word,

or soft as dew a phrase to alight,

transcending craft into expressiveness.

Was expressiveness, genuine and true, in my life?

I remembered when, suddenly it seemed,

training became my own and I knew what to say and do.

I remembered when I became Master of marriage.

And you? Do you find that moment or moments,

or the gradual emergence of yourself

having entered your routines, passions, longings

to express in a more satisfying way your being in the world?

I bet you do.

There is a subtle but distinct perspective
from when I am with you as if we are part of a scheme of things
and when I am with you simply being with you.

I can feel the shift
from holding us aloft within some significance meant to be
to experiencing you right here in the frolic simply as we are.

A subtle but distinct perspective
from husband, wife, nephew, niece,
sister, brother, friend, mother, father, son, daughter,

or treasured portent of purpose to serve,
soul mates,
promise of meeting forever in heaven,

to just you and me enjoying each other
whoever we may be, whatever our destiny.
And I must say, I quite prefer just being here with you.

That slender thread of pleasure in waking to a new day

is as easily broken as the careless swiping away

of the dew-laden, sun-lit gossamer of a spider's web

by thrashing about in anxious thoughts or disappointments.

O, to make a habit

of letting that fragile thread weave a pattern of contentment

along the pathways of the day.

Marie Scott

Slipping from sparkling lights
spun to shades of lavender,
childhood to adulthood
to time having wended its way
to this golden haze of age.

Shifting attention
moves the heart
from longing
to engagement,
looks for change
from the superficial
to causes at root.

Glorious color
the sunrise
to the east.
The west
shadowed
in fading night.
A glance
in each direction.

Shifting attention,
clearing the mind,
moving the heart.

Let me smile upon humanity,
this mass of individuals
orchestrated across the face of the earth,
lives circling in rhythm with the stars,
feeling pain and joy, living fully,
living stunted, frail and helpless,
chatty as birds, sullen as storm clouds,
full of kindness, bullying and hateful.
Let me smile at the flux and flow
of these fascinating, irritating beings
who destroy as much as they create,
who dance as often as stand shattered.
Let me smile upon myself.

Riding the bus is a test in tolerance, it would seem.
How tolerant we are as human beings.
How well we do in close proximity,
within a mix of peoples
all shades of color, varieties of languages,
varying attitudes, coping skills—
levels of tolerance.

There are those who won't ride the bus at all.
There are those who do so begrudgingly,
fearful or critical, closed down, jaw clenched
or mouth open in loud complains,
clutching their bags, ready to take offense.

There are those who relish the mix, relaxed,
enlivened, feel part of the human race,
notice hairstyles, watch with interest
attitudes, personalities, destinations,
make eye contact, smiling.

Tolerantly, intolerantly,
living life right here together
when riding the bus.

If we treat everyone like people we know
in our impersonal to and fro,
I've noticed we bring happiness
we simply mustn't forego.

MARIE SCOTT

Sitting pondering upon the richness

of literature, religion, science,

religions throughout time and across civilization,

it appears,

are containers constructed to hold deep understanding,

then inevitably, falsely, become unto themselves

the sacredness they were constructed to contain.

And literature, too, it would seem, and science,

take on a pomp and circumstance beyond their original inspiration.

That is when revolt of the senses shifts and strains against them,

when religion opens and changes,

science explores more deeply,

literature bursts its bounds

and human life stirs anew.

Or so it seems,

sitting here, pondering.

He lifts and carries away
the heavy bins of dirty dishes
then hauls them back again, clean.
Does he see in me,
sitting here to be served a meal,
a tiresome pile of unwashed dishes?
How could he see me as anything else?
But he catches my eye
and smiles a word of greeting.

MARIE SCOTT

When the renowned Margaret Meade was a child
tied to her schoolroom seat to curb her restless curiosity,
her grandmother took her out of school
and taught her academics and nature, wide and free.

Today, in the name of responsibility and safety,
a classroom of children are tied together and holding hands,
making their way into nature for a "field trip."
Do they ever run free, these children?

What does is mean to be so confined?
What does it mean to the children as children,
to children as they grow up and become adults?
What does it mean to us as a society?

It can't bode well.

Love whispers in the rush of the wind,

in the unfurling of the sea,

in the skittering of the sands on the dunes.

Love sings her song in the night sky

and in the brightness of the day.

She shines golden and warm

in the glow of your tenderness.

Love all around,

making us the best that we can be.

Bees and butterflies,
hummingbirds and robins
fly and flutter, sip nectar,
make my garden home.

There, too, are worms and gophers,
spiders, furry caterpillars, beetles
and other crawly, whirly things.
A whole world different from me.

There are microbes, mites, parasites,
come at my birth,
beneficial symbiotic colonization
living on my skin and inside me.

And me and mine
inhabiting the earth,
part of a solar system, a universe,
gazing in wonder at stars and the moon.
Everything living here together.

It's not easy to slip away—
well, that is, if you're not dying.
If you're dying it's the easiest thing in the world—
one moment you're here, the next you're gone.
Maybe not quite in that order, but the effect is the same—
you've slipped away.

But for the rest of us, it's not so easy.
You can push everyone away
but others always seem to pop up
calling on your time,
your thoughts, your attention,
and there you are—
back again.

Or you hunker down,
close the door, don't answer the doorbell or phone
and listlessly wander around the house.
But eventually, your mind wanders with you
to a thought that leads you to an idea
that carries you somewhere,
and there you are again—
not slipped away.

Life is just too abundant
with trivia, with necessities

and, yes, let's face it,

with enticements and small pleasures.

Seldom, it would seem, the ones we dream of, reach for,

but ones that pull us in nevertheless—

prevent our slipping away.

We keep going, us humans, no matter what, carried along on life's hum,

except for suicides, which keep increasing in number,

except for deadly accidents and mortal illnesses,

except for killings of war and on the streets,

except for natural causes of deaths.

We trudge our way eastward

in opposite trajectory of the sun.

We trudge our way back westward,

standing at waters' edge as the sun sinks into the sea.

Amidst our trudging our thoughts spin,

we greet others, have a social drink or two,

perhaps even make friends, find lovers.

In our trudging we put our hands to tasks,

we spend money, keep up appearances,

we agonize, despair, win small victories.

As we trudge along, we argue and struggle,

hold close our beloveds, pushing and pulling,

disappointing, embracing again.

We are softened and hardened by memories.

And more, although we don't often pause in appreciation,

we dance the dance of life, in our trudging,

we sing the song of living, we shout the joy of abandon,

hear the whispers of breezes, the chirping of insects,

smell the scent of summer and autumn,

love this and that, and each other, despite ourselves,

because we keep going, us humans, no matter what.

The music box played its tinkling tune,

its winding-down sound carrying to the other room.

The moon was pale behind a film of fog.

With the tune came feeling, nostalgic and tender,

nourishing a place not touched

by food or drink, thought or engagement,

or any of the things at play each day.

A soft breath in the mists, a sigh of satisfaction.

When the mundane intrudes on important things,
two paths open:
the flurry of rushing through
and the slowing down to become attentive.
The flurry agitates, lifts to a screeching pitch.
The slowing down quiets, smooths to a flow.

I touch the fabric of the bed sheet I'm folding,
feel its softness, notice its color, smooth its edges.
Of its own accord my breath fills the cavity of my chest,
reaches my belly, my eyes soften.
And I'm here in the brightness of the day
where the mind can follow the heart.

Not to say we want never to hurry,
when quickness in movement exhilarates.

Even when we know what's coming next,

can predict the end of the story,

some of us keep reading.

We can't resist the pulsing of the human heart.

X

Women and Men

How carelessly you
run your fingers through my hair—
How carelessly you
press your lips to mine
wander to the throbbing hollow of my throat.

How carelessly you
lie with legs wrapped 'round me
arms encircling my life—

How carelessly
you steal my heart.

Your view of women and of me is less than who I am.
Expand your vision to embrace me, I said.

Perhaps you hold an exaggerated opinion of your kind, he replied.

You'll never know until you've stopped assuming and
allowed yourself to discover me, I answered.

I was met with silence.

The word of the ages
is that women and men are to be kept apart,
distinct and different from each other.

A new word is out and about
which sings of connection between men and women,
a song of interaction and closeness-in-kind.

Some people are giving the possibilities consideration.

Money, sex, power, he said. That's what makes a man.

Little boys, three and four years old, assault their girl playmates in preschool, reports their teacher. They hit them, knock them down, take away their toys, call them names, taunt and laugh at them. The little girls don't fight back. Little boys act like this toward one or two other little boys, but not all. Little boys exercising power. Little boys learning what makes a man.

Money, sex, power. That's what makes a man? The thought occurs: remove sexual conquest from the formula and the construct falters. Deconstruct the triumvirate and the human beings within it are rescued, this power-construct which dominates humanity is shifted.

In a recent groundswell, women are standing together and saying, "Me Too. I have been sexually harassed, sexually assaulted, raped, and here is who did that to me." Remarkably, the men named are removed from their positions of power, respected men, talented men, men who are admired.

Previously such action against violation was met with blame for those violated, barriers to righting the wrongs were erected, perpetrators of violation were not, as a whole, brought to accountability. This time, the circle usually drawn to protect the violators is not being drawn.

Unprecedented.
Sexual conquest named as sexual misconduct.
The power-construct shifting.

The position of women in society has changed.

Women have taken a place in the public arena.

They have taken a place alongside men in the workplace, the boardrooms.

They are making money and earning power.

It is these women who are speaking out, saying "No More"

to men using positions of power for sexual conquest, as sexual predators.

Could it be that the construct has reached its zenith?

Could it be that a new way for men and women to be together is at hand?

Could it be that sex, money, power shared makes a new man, a new world?

It just could be.

To be a man with strength of arm
to take another human being at will—
What exhilaration. What power.

Intricacies of systems within systems
designed to disguise subordination, brutality, domination.
Whorehouses, dressed in garters and lace,
branding women as outcasts.
On the streets, in board and locker rooms, the titillations,
smirching glances, patting, pinching, remarking, hooting.
Wives and mothers elevated to respectability
under control, body and soul, of head-of-household.

Or in the dark of night, all else aside,
to grab hold and straightforwardly rape.
Ah, to be a man!

Irrelevant,

it would seem,

our pleas for humanity,

for respect between men and women,

the art of seeing one another,

caring about one another.

Irrelevant when Rape With Robots is for sale.

Oh, our pleas evermore urgent.

How is it that inventors, manufacturers

and advertisers of robots-for-rape

are not convicted of hate crimes?

"Women need men
like fish need a bicycle"
was the shout heard round the world,
a rallying cry.

But, O, that shiny bicycle
with silver handlebars
and colorful tassels!

What women don't need
is men's domination, control.
What women don't need
is subjection to men's distain.
What women don't need
is men's predatory
sexual harassment,
assault, rape.
What women don't need
is men's physical,
emotional and verbal
battering.
What women don't need
is men's violence,
men's proclivity for war.
What women don't need
is men's condescension,

men's barring women from
equal rights, equal opportunities.
What women don't need
is men's assumed superiority.
What women don't need
is to be dependent on men
or subservient to them.
What women don't need
is to rely on men
more than on herself.
What women don't need
is to replace her thoughts with his.

And that shiny bicycle?
O, women want
men's love, men's smell,
men's bodies to meet theirs.
Women want men
to see them, respect them,
desire their thoughts and opinions,
talk with them as equals,
walk with them side by side.
Women want men
to live in the same
not a separate world.
Women want men
to stand tall beside them,
wrap their arms around them,
point to ways true and sound,

and see clearly where women are pointing.
Women want men
to love them
and they want to love men.

Women want to ride that bicycle
on streets broad and winding,
through puddles splashing their ankles.
Women want to ride that bicycle
with wind in their hair.
Women want to toil and sweat
riding to mountaintops.
Women want to ride
laughing, shouting, holding tight,
racing ahead, lagging behind.
Women want to ride that bicycle
down country lanes and lie down in
meadows of wildflowers.
Women want to ride the bicycle
of women and men
in companionship, adventure,
all of life's challenges and joys.

O, women need men
like men need women
to make this world
the world we want
to live in together.

Marie Scott

Freud's psychology convinced generations
that women's reports of rape by family members and strangers
were really female hysteria, penis envy.

A century later therapists were discredited, losing licenses to practice,
when helping patients to recover childhood memories of rape,
calling the violence by name, by perpetrator.

But now! Oh, now!
Adult women have gone viral as #MeToo
remembering sexual abuse.

Gone viral to change the culture
of the rape of girls and boys, of women,
naming men as responsible for their criminal sexual violence.

A new time has come to call it out.
Call it out to end it.

They stared in disbelief; they shouted their innocence,
these men in powerful places. They said it wasn't true,
when the women rose up and said, "No more."
No more sexual harassment, sexual assault, rape.
We'll bring you down. And they did.

They howled, their faces contorted with rage, they stamped their feet.
They wailed, "You just want us to be like women!"
when the women said, "And more."
Sexual prowess will no longer dictate your manhood,
orchestrate your power, lead you around by the nose.
You'll integrate your sexuality into your personhood.

Their wails ceased as they became men instead of aggressors,
when their maleness shone sensuous, bright and free,
when they looked upon women with respect and genuine affection,
when passion between them became mutual,
when women said, "At last."

Safely women turned their smiles upon the men
in the once-dark corridors inhabited by chambermaids,
in the once-vulnerability of women's occupations,
on campuses, in the bedroom, before cameras,
in the halls of government, in the boardroom.

Everywhere. A new day. A new time.

MARIE SCOTT

I love men.
I love their stance in the world.
They look as if they belong in it.
I emulate this.

I love their shape, their sinew,
the flatness of their belly,
the lean strength of their forearms.
I adore it.

I love the incredible softness and power
of the organ by which they identify.
I love that it's theirs.
I love their sharing it with me.

I love the sound of their voices,
the way they smile, their warm glances.
It feels good when they notice me.
It feels good to notice them.

I love how different from me,
how they bring a new energy,
and yet how still of me
that they are.

I love men
when they're themselves,

relaxed and whole,
a fellow human being.

In true love, of course,
there is the current of subtleties.

The waters gather in a rush,
forming sweeps of grandeur.

The bends in the river
form eddies of quiet waters.

The dance of the waves,
rush forward, swirl backward.

The wind blowing upstream,
ruffles the waters racing toward it.

Toss the coursing subtleties onto
the stern pavements and pathways of living life,
splash these waters against the buttresses
of expectations and demands,
and true love stumbles, thirsts.

It is then that lovers must hold still,
listen to the movement of the current,
the depths of the waters, the lay of the land
and the pulse of the heart.

Stand still and listen carefully,

sometimes walking the streets at midnight,

holding their breath and sinking to the bottom of the sea,

looking squarely into the face of the beloved,

casting a sideways glance,

catching glimpses at the corner of the eye.

But always, always,

true love flows with the subtleties,

lets surprises teach new dimensions,

lets disappointments transcend immediacy,

feeds their sweet selves with love.

With the infestation of patriarchy
buzzing and chirping on our skin,
how will we ever know each other?

In a soft summer evening
smelling of honeysuckle and cinnamon
with the stars and the moon smiling down,
will you cross your ankle on your knee
and expound on your accomplishments?
From making love and plans,
your eyes bright and warm,
your hands soft and tender,
will you smirk a condescending, "Yes, dear"
when I make a serious request?
In giving birth to children
and singing together life's sweet song
will you shrug when I talk to you?
In conversation with friends,
will you give me a look,
covertly touch my arm,
monitor my participation?
If you hold me, your beloved, apart,
stepped slightly back from me,
willing to demean me
without knowing you do,
hold me as Other,

how will we as a people

stop creating wars,

quit abuse and transgressions?

How will we ever know to together

smell honeysuckle and cinnamon,

smile back at the stars and the moon?

If you take a moment each day to see me

and if I do the same for you,

perhaps the shining stars will drop us

into a tumbling, tangled heap of sweet

honeysuckle, cinnamon and moonlight.

If when I make a request of you,

you seriously take it into consideration,

and if I do the same for you,

perhaps we will expand

and wrap our arms around each other.

If you do not wish to meet my request,

you speak openly and sincerely to me,

and if I do the same for you,

perhaps the grand discovery of being true to ourselves

while embracing another will be ours.

If when I talk you listen,

wanting to deeply understand,

and if I do the same for you,

perhaps our hearts will open,

we will feel more whole and sure of ourselves,

we will not feel so alone

with the world pressing up against us.
If you let me be me when we're in company,
let me stand on my own for better or worse,
and if I do the same for you,
perhaps we'll see the good and the bad of us,
and laugh a laugh of acceptance.
If you hold me, your beloved,
as part of you, as equal to you,
and if I do the same for you,
perhaps we will dance with joy
for all the world to see.

And, oh happy thought,
we will also be swatting
pesky patriarchal bugs off our skin!

XI

We Are All In It Together

Cultures change within our lifetimes.

Before our very eyes, though barely perceptible.

We see fathers nurturing their children,

changing diapers, cuddling, talking baby-talk.

We see women taking positions in public leadership.

We see everyone eating more fruits and vegetables

and moving their bodies for fitness.

We recognize the preciousness of the environment.

See a mix of color among people residing together.

See people smile and step aside to let wheelchairs pass by,

and buses built to lower their step-up for the aging and infirm.

And we're almost not able to remember when all this wasn't so.

All on the same corner.
A man with a bedroll, homeless,
making his way slowly along the walkway.
A young woman jogging,
her dog alongside her, his tongue lolling.
An older man, taking his morning walk.
Two tourists checking Google maps on smart phones
and looking appreciatively at the landscape.

None on the same corner seem to notice the others.
The homeless, the young, the old, tourists,
all passing each other without seeing.
Without seeing lives in such differing circumstance,
people with such varying experiences
sharing space but not connection,
a richness of life unregistered.

All the while
the roadways crisscross, nature stands vigil.

I sit at the window of the cafe
secure in my own private world,
eating strawberries and sipping coffee,
watching the lives passing by.
I think of the existences among strangers
which we are all living on this corner or on another,

wondering, if it were different would we be kinder,
more embracing of all that's around us,
more seeing of each other.

And if it were different,
if the young woman dare smile at the homeless man
without fear of aggression,
if the homeless man touched the older man's elbow
assisting him up the stairs without fear of distain,
if they knew in their hearts
that each was an extension of themselves,
would the world shift, rotate more slowly,
give time for reflection and home to compassion,
all on the same corner or on another.

We're calling on authorities to keep us safe,
neighbors who know each other,
who trust each other, who like each other,
who live on a quiet street in expensive houses.

A quiet street until we hear shouts
and a distant gun shot in the night,
until we see trash at the bottom of the hill
where people have slept in vans,
until we find needles and drug paraphernalia at Lands End,
that wondrous land touching the sea,
until the homeless ask for food, money,
and dare walk our sidewalks,
who live, if you can call it that,
hidden in the forest and hillside we cherish.

We're calling on authorities to protect us
from the unthinkable horror of an underworld
we want covered from view, pushed far, far away from us.
We don't want to face what's brought them here,
these human beings who are human beings just like us,
"fallen" we say, on hard times.
Or, we say, derelicts "choosing" to destroy themselves
along with all we hold dear.

We don't want to face that we're in this together.

MARIE SCOTT

That these we now fear and view with disgust
are now our neighbors.

Authorities have not been successful
in protecting against the encroachment
across our country, across our city, now across our lives.
Where do we look if we don't look only to the authorities,
to thinking better lighting and more regular patrol will keep us safe,
believing there's somebody else who will fix this problem?

We don't know where to look. We don't know who to ask.
We don't have a way to think about this
except to be afraid and call for help.
But we must.
We must think deeper than protection.
We must think better than anybody's thought before.

We must ask ourselves if we neighbors
facing together what's happening to us
can perhaps be a cluster of intelligence and compassion
who will invent a solution beyond "them" and "us."
We may be neighbors who are willing to look deeply
at what surely is systemic with causes beyond the individual.
We may be neighbors who are willing
to look into practices, policies, culture
which have served us well, some of us at least
—until now—
when how we've structured our society left out too many.

It will take courage, compromise, time and energy.
It will take what none of us wish to give,
resistance to the deep ebb within us which
only wants to rely on authority.

I write this. But I know within myself
that I feel no impulse strong enough to move me from complacency.
I want to close my eyes, close my mind, and keep pretending.
Pretending that all is well, that this is just a passing thing.

But here it is.
It's not going to go away.
Now it's spoken,
this more pervasive threat we're up against,
the unreconciled odds we're avoiding to rectify.

When a white man is on trial
he is seen as someone who has acted illegally.

When a woman of any color is on trial
she is seen as deceitful, manipulative.

When a black man is on trial
he is seen as violent, untrustworthy.

When a poor white man is on trial
he is seen as a lowlife.

These subtleties in our attitudes, unrecognized,
breed racism, sexism, classism.

Honey-colored skin,
an aquiline nose,
eyes, dark pools
of an ancient people
sitting right here on the bus beside me!
What privilege to have the world come to our doorstep.

Some of us had nervous breakdowns
and didn't know why.
Some of us stepped into line
discounted, lesser-than.
Some of us fell by the wayside.
Some of us became clear-eyed
and birthed a movement for justice.
So sing a song of compassion,
a song of victory,
a song of women's minds and hearts,
of women treading long paths to citizenship,
to personhood, to inclusion in humanity,
to rising through murky waters
to verve and hallowed ground of timeless change,
goodness and freedom and betterment for all.

We genuinely have it all,

the love, the passion, the attraction.

We just don't know how to reach the heart of it

and connect there,

we people.

If everyday cruelties
were made physical,
we'd all be outfitted
in tourniquets and bandages.

It's not enough for the trill of birdsong to carry us along.

It's not enough for the majesty of mountains to thrill us.

It's not enough for the ocean's sweep to fill us with delight.

We must bring song and majesty and delight

into the living moments of every life.

We must re-think our ways of being people

so that song and majesty and moon-swelled waters

carry us each and every one, each and every day

into lives rich in wonder, wrapped in well-being.

We must make birdsong and mountains the mainstay,

the daily bread where none go hungry,

where none live in fear, where violence is extinct.

We must. We can.

We changed terrain in a hefty effort of speaking injustice.
Landscaping remains to be done,
clearing toppled buildings,
planting gardens,
molding our "Spaceship Earth"
to receive new architecture which houses all,
a garden which excludes no one from nourishment,
no species neglected, no ecology ignored.

We dived deep into the psyche of humanity
exposing this and making visible that,
taking all the systems of thought, all the beliefs
and mulling them over
to reach a fuller dimension of understanding.

I say "we"
but I stood on the sidelines
cheering, marveling,
grateful to those whose raised voices spoke eloquently,
whose strong bodies strode masterfully,
whose guiding intelligence clarified,
stirring our consciousness, lifting our spirits.

Kin are emerging who earlier went unrecognized.
Vistas are opening which once were unperceived.
Old prejudices erupt, spilling hatred,

as new energies flood in.
Old power is clung to
as eyes turned elsewhere erodes its hold.

We're babies learning to walk,
arms outstretched,
babbling sounds becoming words,
wobbly steps steadying into running and skipping.
An age-old occurrence
this breaking into new,
into better and worse all at once.

So here we are.
In this span of time,
we're taking our moment
to open our eyes and hearts.

Hatred contains as many nutrients as love.
We can feed off it indefinitely.

What we have to do is choose.
Choose to live out of hatred or from love.

The way we can live from love is to
find a way to get through our hurt.

This is as true for ourselves and lovers
as it is for terrorists.

Perhaps the crimes of humanity
are building once again to a crescendo,
a fireworks of change
as in my younger years, that moment of social foment
erupting in movement for peace, for civil rights,
for women's liberation, for gay and lesbian rights,
toward recognition of and inclusive privilege
for every disenfranchised people in our rich country,
a movement of expanding consciousness
built on years and years of hundreds and hundreds of tiny groups
and millions of voices raised against injustice.

Perhaps a moment happening again, now,
in the midst of hateful power struggles, blatant distortions, violence,
reactions fueled by irrational fears against including everyone,
efforts to silence what cannot be quieted.
Voices raised to say we can all prosper,
we can see our way to peace and justice for all,
be considerate of one another and the earth.

Is the course of history once again on the move
in its perpetual rhythm toward greater possibilities,
tiny moves demanding, responding, interacting,
fueling the direction for change,
the subtle, mighty, vulnerable, infinitesimal turning,
humanity ever reaching toward what we know we can be,

articulating the wonder of it, elated to be witness to it.

Perhaps the crimes of humanity

are building once again to a crescendo for change.

"Teaching English
Connecting People"
the slogan on the t-shirt read.

For greater connection,
I thought,
it could read

"Teaching English
Learning French/Italian/Arabic/Mandarin/
Hindi/Russian/Spanish/Portuguese
Connecting People"

A Thought Form here,
alerting me to pay attention.

Thought Forms, subtle messengers
to our hearts and minds,
shaping our connections,
influencing perceptions,
propelling cultures,
speaking to us,
while we speak
to each other.

We as a people,
by paying attention

to Thought Forms,
can pay attention
to shaping them
shaping us.

Let your tenderness come out to play.
Let your lips grow soft and full with kisses.
Let your heart open when you catch my eye.
Let your body fold around mine in sweet embrace.

Look at the sparkle in the sunshine.

Against tyranny of the powerful,
Against the violence that's hammering us,
Against harm to humanity,
Against our own weaknesses twisting us.

See the sparkle in the waves on a cloudy day.

For such is a lilting song
Of something more
Of something beyond
Of something for a new tomorrow.

See the sparkle in the sunshine and in the waves on a cloudy day.

Let the tenderness of us all come out to play.
Let eyes soften and meet among strangers.
Let smiles grace our lips as we pass by.
Let love warm our talk.

MARIE SCOTT

This species has trounced every inch of my skin.
Didn't like it, but I was tolerating it.
Now they've sent their poisons into my atmosphere.
I thought the age of the dinosaur was bad,
but this, I can't let it continue.

The sun and moon and stars all say
there is an intelligence within this species
compatible with the whole of life. I sense it, too.
But you'd never know it!
We're left with no alternative but to put a stop to them.

I'm hearing them moan and wail
at the ferociousness of the storms
sent by wind and snow and ice,
at the rising tides, at the burning swaths of land.

But will they curb their birth rate?
Will they change their habits of transportation
or their fascination with the endless string of inventions
wrecking my generous supply of resources?
Will they resolve their differences with one another
and stop bombing my fragile body?

No. And it's gone on so long
that it will be centuries before we can heal ourselves.

Heal the rent in the stratosphere.

Heal the chopping down of my forests.

Heal the greed and violence of their behaviors.

Heal ourselves, we will, however,

for that is our instructions within universe,

while uppity species come and go.

Hate to see this frolicking, appealing group extinct,

but what recourse do we have?

Here's one way how it may be happening,
these divides between the powerful and the rest of us.
It suddenly seems so clear:
it's where attention lies, where intention is set.

There's those whose job it is to live life responsibly,
keeping a career, raising a family.
There's those whose job it is to run companies for profit,
or to govern nations defined in institutional terms.

Those providing for themselves and family
are working hard to make ends meet,
are busy with children after a day's work,
with the ins and outs of daily life.

Company heads and heads of state
are focused on running the company or the country,
a whole different world from the rest of us
an entirely different schema.

That the two collide is inevitable,
agendas being so different,
energies and accomplishments
moving in circles within circles.

What is good for companies
and for heads of state to be heads of state

does not relate to you and me
despite the rhetoric to the contrary.

Those who are elected to keep the country running,
those who are assigned to a capitalist economy,
operate on terms irrespective of human lives,
committed to political and economic agencies.

Folks attending to their individual lives
within the structures of country and business
can only be lost in the shuffle,
incidentally and randomly included in the good for all.

Democracy is polarized. Democracy has to be restructured.
But who is to do it?
Folks whose energies and commitments are to life and living?
Those whose success lies in the given structures?

Can attention be shifted between the two?
Can intention be unified?
Important questions.
Elusive answers.

A slender man
a smiling woman,
world leaders:
President of the United States,
Secretary of State.

President Elect,
a goat, curled horns butting, bullying.
Dominance or cooperation,
which, my people, will we choose?

North and center, south, east, west
the goat has trotted
cheating, cajoling, manipulating,
finding foothold on the rocky ledges of the world.

The fellow-goat residing in the north
trampling countries around him,
threatening the borders of free people,
butting heads with our goat, romping, playful.

How is it that our goat
will play with that goat,
the people cried!

It's their game
spoke the voice within us.

They're the bad boys in the schoolyard
seeing how far they can go
marking their turf, gaining control.
So beware, O, my people.
You'll pay their dues.
That's their game.

Bombast. Bullying.
An excitability, a frenzy among us.
A stirring of the deeps,
flotsam and jetsam floating to the surface.

We see it in our crowded hustle and bustle,
tense frowns, eyes darting.
We see it in our art.
We see it in the shootings on our streets,
killings by the protectors of the people,
killings of the people by the people.
We see it in hostilities between groups of us.
We see it in male aggression,
sexual harassment, assault, rape,
males separating their sexuality from their hearts, from humanity.
We see it in the faces of those fleeing war, famine, brutality,
hundreds of thousands, millions.

We see it.
We huddle together. We stay indoors.
We take to the streets in protest.
We text. We petition.
We sit in restaurants and decry our plight.
We write poems.

And still, the bullying continues,
policies pit us against each other, harm is done,

destruction of our precious earth is fostered,
the air we breathe polluted.
And still, the bombast increases in volume,
shouting profanities, blaming, coercing, controlling,
exciting a frenzy among us.

Trust shaken.
Sweetness, caring, loving tremble
in the bombast, in the bullying.

Don't speak to me of God,
I've done time in that fabrication.

Don't speak to me of democracy,
I'm informed of its deficiencies.

Don't speak to me of families,
I've witnessed their cruelties.

Don't speak to me of society
constructed of systems within systems,
sustaining some, crushing others,
fostering prejudices, divisiveness, turmoil,
holding the world together, pulling it apart.

Don't speak to me of empires,
we all know how they rise and fall.

Speak to me of something real
to ease my aching heart.

Speak to me of justice and compassion
that includes us all.

Speak to me of love
however elusive.

Speak to me
as we do time here together.

THIS IS A TRUE STORY

He was a murderer, a vicious murderer,

stabbing to death two women,

stabbing them multiple times.

As was considered just,

a jury of twelve condemned him to death.

Then the jury of twelve, none of them murderers,

went home from doing their duty

and were forever haunted

by condemning to death another person,

no matter how just.

The weather. Ah, the weather.

Weather speaking by way of climate

just may be the force of nature

to cause us to reconsider our assumptions.

Jesus sported a long black beard, hook nose, brown skin. Remember, it's not the whiskers to be feared or revered, it's the man within.

Fascism is afoot,

that meandering menace,

that megalomaniac political force gorging on power,

that recurring Thought Form in its various guises.

The current megalomaniac

does not identify itself with history,

thinks itself new and righteous.

But it's as old as patriarchy,

when power over others became attractive

and entrenched itself within humankind,

just as destructive in all its portent of building civilizations,

built and then torn down by the very weight that lifted them into existence.

So let's recognize it,

this menace again in our midst.

And let us recognize the truly new

—or perhaps the only truly ancient—

which is also recurring,

where all people have voice

and a politic forms inclusive of us all.

Is there a way for wars to cease?

When men nurtured in competition,

girded with pride of power and strength of arm,

are joined by women nurtured in softness and compliance,

is there a flow in the halls of governance for warmth and embrace?

Or will the corrosive pressures of the ranks they've joined

bend the will of women to the ways of men?

We stand at a threshold.

Refugees from war-torn nations surge into realms holding reign.

People of every race and from far-flung lands mingle.

The Thought Form of democracy asserts itself against the idea of tyrannical rule.

Economies become interdependent globally.

Distribution of wealth is demanded to be equitable.

None is in place, yet,

no river courses or flood plains are yet carved to include us all,

but the flow is begun,

spring sources are gushing sweet waters.

Can we follow its bubbling freshness until battles look foolish?

Can we harken the moment and change the course of time?

Can we learn the way not yet taken, we multitudes of mingling peoples?

Green fields paved over,

vast lands entombed beneath high-rise buildings,

the melting ice caps, her tears,

gales and rising water, her fury.

Her despair sweeps the deserts dry.

Her distress bursts forests into flame.

We run from her demise

having covered the globe with disregard.

And there is no place to hide.

And yet—

there was Noah's flood

and other colossal disasters

with life thereafter.

But thereafter to disaster may just be stories

springing from our anxieties, our precipitated annihilation,

buried guilt of our misadventures.

And yet—

in the complexities, the intricacies,

in boundless possibilities,

there may lie nuanced layers of promise.

There may be hope.

It was an era of self-congratulation.

We had won independence as a nation, as a people.

We had instituted democracy like never before.

We had freed the enslaved.

We had helped rescue Europe from tyranny.

We were the greatest nation on earth,

the finest, most just and admirable people.

It was an era of exposure.

The wormholes in the woodwork began to show.

Our attempted genocide.

Our bullying and destabilizing smaller nations.

Our destruction of our planet, albeit unintentional.

Our warmongering.

Our violence against people of color for not being white.

Our raping, murdering of women, domestic violence.

Our striving for wealth and power-over

instead of democracy's power-of.

Greed and fear of weakness

over-ruling the good for all and the health of the lands.

It is an era of reckoning.

A time for making good the era of praise,

making good our constitutional intention of

"We the People of the United States,

in Order to form a more perfect Union, establish Justice,

ensure domestic Tranquility, provide for the common Defense,

promote the general Welfare, and secure the Blessing of Liberty

for ourselves and our Posterity."

A time to make good our Declaration of Independence

"that all men [meaning all people] are created equal...

with unalienable rights, that among these are

life, liberty, and the pursuit of happiness."

A time for owning up to hurts and horrors,

learning their causes and perpetrations.

A time to exercise the muscle of our moral fiber.

A time of conscience dawning on our consciousness.

A time to change our ways, open our heart, expand our intelligence,

make real the true goodness we profess.

A time that is now.

When the line begins to curve
and right angles no longer apply.
When the mind takes flight
and begins to circle the globe.
When societal norms waver
and institutions are examined.
When the earth begins to melt
and the world goes topsy-turvy.
Then we begin to talk to one another.
We open our hearts, search our soul....
Others of us have to run for our lives.

There's so much we can't do,
we ordinary citizens,
that collectively others do.

We can't predict the weather days in advance.
We can't build the engine to fly to the moon or Mars.
We can't concoct the remedies to cure our ills.
We can't assure our safety in a ravaged world.
We don't truly know how our government is run
and what we do know is troubling.
We don't understand how wealth is accrued
but we know it's constructed to be divisive.
With computers installed, we can't even fix our own cars.

What we can do,
in the midst of all this magic, all this wonder and strife,
what we can do, caught up in all that's beyond our control,
is love one another.
Who knows how we know to do this, but we do,
and we can remember to.

One child only, they said,
and people were forced to comply.
Contraception is a sin, they said,
and children continued to multiply.
Plan your family as you see fit, they allowed,
and choice spread across the land.
No matter what the policy, the population grew,
grew to numbers that set the earth to groaning,
set societies straining in the face of too many,
too fast, too converging and closely packed.

So we tumble over one another,
we fight for sustenance, material and emotional,
as resources dwindle and climate changes,
as distress mounts with no solutions in sight,
we numerous, numerous people,
we people so dear to ourselves.

Young white men, mostly, marching,
hatred distorting their handsome faces,
carrying shields painted with swastikas
brandishing clubs and knives and guns
proclaiming white supremacy
shouting ugly epitaphs denouncing
Jews, anyone not white, not Christian.

The shame, ignorance,
atrocity of such proclamation
in the face of a shattering history
to which we've all been privy.

Back, brown, white people, hundreds,
stand with placards depicting
hooded men burning crosses,
lynched black men and women,
emaciated Jews in death camps.
Lining the roadside of these marchers, witnesses
softly, fiercely, murmuring "never again."
Never again!
Never again!

We lived in a time of its glory.
We live in a time of its demise.

Our empire
like all empires before it
may be dying.

May it die gracefully.

May the birth to come
cradle a civilization
that wraps it arms around us all.

What I read stirred the blood and the imagination.

I must keep a copy of this!

So I began to loosen the page from the magazine.

It resisted. I tugged, careful not to damage the whole.

Persistently, I turned the edge of the page this way and that.

Gently, forcefully loosened its hold.

At last, that first small separation of page from book.

Then with ease, it pulled free.

As I held the page in my hand, I thought how like

oppression, discrimination, injustice, hatefulness, poverty,

when earnestly loosened, come free, release into the hands

of new hope, new life, new world.

Great numbers of people
are putting their humanity
into efforts of outrageous good-will,
creating vibrant works of change
in the chasms overlooked by greed and prejudice.

A persisting line of demarcation after all this time

from when enslaved dark-skinned people were set free,

a line where white-skinned people like you and me

still put our hand in front of our mouths, lower our voice and whisper,

"she was black, but…"

"he was…well, you know, black…"

Don't we see it? Don't we hear it?

This persisting line of separation

perpetuating harm, dissension, injustice, violence

against those people with a different skin color

these we've separated out for no good reason whatsoever?

When will we abolish such a reckless, useless, imaginary line between us?

It's way past time.

If we see images other than
beautiful women gazing up adoringly
at handsome men they lean against,

If we see ordinary-looking men and women
arm-in-arm happily smiling at each other,

If we see women in various poses
actively standing on their own,
a welcomed part of things,

If we see two men kissing,
two women looking into each other's eyes,
two men and two women obviously in love,

If we see heterosexual and homosexual older couples,
If we see older women and men on their own living eager lives,

If we see the poor, the rich, the in-between
with equal frequency, with equal respect,

If we see the range of color among us,

If all of us in our many aspects are represented
among the visual images splashed across our consciousness,

Life is more real. We feel more a part of things.

Where is the heartbeat
of the heart of the people,
a beat steady and strong
that makes a land whole?

Where is the heartbeat
of the heart of the people
where the heart
beats rhythms of justice?

Syncopated now the heartbeat
of the heart of the people,
a beat of new sounds,
new faces,

brown hearts beating, black,
all-white hearts no longer
owning the drumming,
new hands drumming new songs.

A dance freed,
the heartbeat of the heart of the people
blending sounds, thrumming rhythms,
for a land that is whole.

MARIE SCOTT

IN APPRECIATION

Tami Schlies is my niece and a successful author who publishes on her own. She told me I might do the same, and her enthusiasm and expertise inspired me to pursue bringing this book of poems to press. My warm and loving appreciation.

Tami recommended her editor, Kellie Doherty. As is the way with excellent editors, Kellie has seen to grammatical corrections, made sure the poems are readable, added refinement and pizzaz to my words. Thank you so much, Kellie.

My frustration with the technical aspects of publishing on my own brought me to Dorrance Publishing Company, a publishing service which assists authors in getting their writing into print. Their personable and professional assistance has put this book into your hands. Thank you for your invaluable help and for your generosity in holding my hand.

Cynthia Green, my niece, instigated the cover for this book. She researched images and artists. Her love, enthusiasm, delight, clever ideas and unerring good taste prompted its design. Without her initiation it would never have come to be. Without her, an element of fun would be missing!

Nicole. Of course! Remember her gorgeous poppies? She's the artist for us! Nicole Calder, heart-to-heart friend of both Cynthia and me, the perfect artist to join our joyful enterprise. She has given visual inspiration and meaning to the words within the cover. Her fun-loving spirit joining us in the project has enriched it greatly.   Her friendship is immeasurable.

A special thanks to Ron Coulter for being such a good friend and for not only encouraging me to write, but for taking the time and attention to thoughtfully read poems as they came into being, giving me honest and insightful feedback. I'm forever grateful.

To Karla Boyd who declared me a poet in the pleasant times we read our poetry aloud to each other, critiquing, giving comment and praise.

To Kelly Yost Hove, musician extraordinaire, for her enthusiasm for putting my poems in print and for her loving embrace of me, always.

To my sisters, Beverly Green, Louise Luton, Ruth Smith for their cheerful listening to poems I shared with them, and just because they are my beloved sisters.

A special thanks to Mollie and Glenda of *BookWomen* for encouraging me to publish the poems and who inspire me by their own work and lives.